WORLD LITERATURE
IN TRANSLATION

THE BURDEN
OF SUFFERANCE

Women Poets of Russia

by
PAMELA PERKINS
and
ALBERT COOK

GARLAND PUBLISHING, INC.
NEW YORK & LONDON 1993

Library of Congress Cataloging-in-Publication Data
Perkins, Pamela, 1955–
    The burden of sufferance : women poets of Russia / by Pamela Perkins
and Albert Cook.
            p.   cm. — (World literature in translation ; v. 19)
    Translated from Russian.
    Includes bibliographical references.
    1. Russian poetry—Women authors—Translations into English. 2. Women
poets, Russian. 3. Russian poetry—Women authors—History and criticism.
I. Cook, Albert Spaulding. II. Title. III. Series: World literature in translation ; 19.
ISBN 0-8240-3325-6
PG3237.E5P47   1993
891.71009'09287—dc20   92-10597

Printed on acid-free, 250-year-life paper
Manufactured in the United States of America

To the Poets of the Stalin Era

Out of the well of your wastes what
Has drawn you has drawn me,
The firm, drowning
Syllables, a lake,
A grave, a wretched
Room-dimness, faces turned away,
All thumbs
Down.

A.C.

Acknowledgments

Although Pamela Perkins is primarily responsible for everything in this volume but the treatment of Akhmatova and Gippius, done by Albert Cook (except for Perkins' translation of *Requiem* and the two short poems for Tsvetaeva), we have looked over each other's work and benefited from expert advice, notably from Victor Terras and Sam Driver (who are by no means responsible for errors of ours that remain). We are further grateful for constant wise help in translating to Irina Mirsky-Zayas, and to Blossom Steinberg Kirschenbaum for resourceful advice and support. And finally, Pamela Perkins does not want this book to appear without her expressions of gratitude to her mother, the late Alexandra Locke Perkins, and her aunt, the late Sonya Locke Reilly.

Contents

Introduction

"There is no woman's question in art . . ."[1]

Marina Tsvetaeva

"Je ne crois pas à l'inconscience d'êtres
pensants, encore moins—d'êtres pensants
écrivants, point du tout—à l'inconscience
écrivaine feminine."

Marina Tsvetaeva
Lettre à l'Amazone [2]

I: The Double Bind of the Russian Woman Poet

Invited by the poet Valeri Briusov to read at an "Evening of Poet-esses" in 1920, Marina Tsvetaeva was not inspired by the occasion and she asked Adalis, the poet who conveyed the invitation, whether one of the other participants was a Communist. When Adalis replied, "Well, woman's communism," Tsvetaeva responded: "I agree that man's monarchism is better . . . But joking aside, is she a Party member or not?" When Adalis replied that she wasn't, Tsvetaeva then asked if the evening was entirely outside of the Party before she would agree to attend. Tsvetaeva's remarks speak to the fundamental contradictions posed by the unifying subject of this collection. The great poet's humorous disdain was rooted in her sensitivity, at once anti-Soviet and anti-political, as well as her scorn for the idea of "woman's verse." Indeed, with her characteristic sound-play, Tsvetaeva found this event to be an "exhibiting" of a woman poet in a cliched and conventional manner instead of a "reading."

1

In his opening remarks at the "Evening of Poetesses," Briusov emphasized "Woman. Love. Passion." Irked, Tsvetaeva instead presented her own four immediate goals: "1.) reading seven poems by a woman without the personal pronoun 'I' or the word 'love,'" 2.) testing the senselessness of poems for the public, 3.) having an exchange with just one person (even a cadet!) who understands; and, 4.)—most important—fulfilling, in Moscow 1921, *a debt of honor.* And aside from goals, the aimless . . . simple and extreme feeling of 'and well?'" Then, to an audience that included Red Army soldiers, in a voice of desperation and bravado, as if "she flew from a mountain" she read poems in praise of the Tsar and the heroism and bravery of the White Army soldiers.

A collection based on gender inevitably underscores the double bind[3] of the poet who remains a woman although she transcends the confines of "ladies' verse" to attain a position on a par with the best male poets of her generation. One risks presenting the kind of collection that Anna Akhmatova anticipated, called "Women of the Time," featuring her with Gippius and others, where "without fail they will find in us a common style." [4] Indeed, to find a common style in these poets would be as impossible as linking Mandelshtam and Mayakovsky; in contrast to Akhmatova, Gippius wrote virtually all of her poetry with a male persona. Tsvetaeva remarked that a poet should also be considered in the light of his or her epoch. In this respect the lives and works of these writers are displaced in this anthology, viewed out of the context of the era and its literary movements. Tsvetaeva and Akhmatova belong in anthologies with Pasternak and Mandelshtam, more than they do with Pavlova or "poetesses" of the nineteenth century.

To attempt to generalize about the Russian woman poet is to enter a minefield. The complexities of the lives and poetry of these writers challenge western feminist criticism, not only in the radically chic mystique of psychoanalytical theory, such as Julia Kristeva's simplistic and erroneous remarks about Tsvetaeva,[5] but in other conclusions drawn about the relationship of literary genius to women's historical position. One cannot assume that because of historical oppression, women have held a marginal position in relation to the world and the literary word without oversimplifying the situation of the woman poet in Russia, before and after the Revolution.

Although Russia's second great age of poetry coincided with educational reforms parallel to those in England, it was still a highly patriarchal society, where, however, women entered the mainstream of the arts. Women played a significant role in the revolutionary movements, more so than they did even after the Revolution. And in Russia, women were key players in the diverse groups of artists during the cultural revolution of the first decades of the twentieth century. Not only poets, but such now valued painters as Natalia Goncharova (1881–1962), Liubov Popova (1889–1924), and Sonia Delaunay (1885–1979)[6], among many others, stood at the forefront of modernism. Even in the nineteenth-century Pavlova published before her marriage. Tsvetaeva, Akhmatova and Gippius all published when they were extremely young, and by 1920 both Tsvetaeva and Akhmatova were well-known. In the twenties critics from both the Formalist camp and the Party used Akhmatova and Mayakovsky as opposite examples of the direction taken by poetry. And in 1925 Akhmatova was named in an article in *Pravda* as the greatest Russian poet since the death of Blok.

Their fates sound a tragic chord and point to yet another irony of Soviet history. Writers and artists were silenced by the censorship and policies of a Marxist government in praxis, a regime with an ideological mandate for progress and for feminism. The first government in the world that alone in principle resolved the classic woman's question, decades later expelled the four editors of the first *samizdat* feminist journal.[7] Paradoxically, women were given employment in the work force on the principles of a new equality, yet they were and still are asked to add age-old feminine drudgery to their other tasks in a society that lacks even the most basic goods. All this against the background of that figure of propaganda, the Soviet superwoman, the image of the Russian woman as a strong, indomitable survivor.

Though a number of the women painters abandoned a more metaphysical and abstract art and joined in the post-revolutionary Soviet organizations, along with the majority of the male artists, the most significant women poets of the early twentieth century, Akhmatova, Tsvetaeva and Gippius, variously maintained an essential distance between politics and poetry. Their aesthetics was markedly different from that of Adrienne Rich, or any post-modern feminist poet. As Xenia Gasiorowska points out in "Women and Russian Literature,"[8] these modernist poets were not interested in emancipation in their works; they did not carry the banners of liberation. As poets, however, they were fully liberated. Karolina Pavlova was the first to address the woman's question on a complex level as an early advocate of woman's education and right to a profession; however as Barbara Heldt points out, she voiced a mix of disdain for women's verse and ambivalence about her gender in her novel *A Double Life.*[9] The novel reflected the opinion that education was essential to a woman writer, plus the fact that the privileged aristocratic young lady had superlative tutorship at home in literature and foreign languages. But it also shows that progress for women in the political and social sphere did not necessarily mark advances in the literary arena, or arguably even more so vice versa. This landmark text for feminist scholarship on the double life of poet and woman was published in Russia in 1848, a year of revolution in Europe, the year of the publication of the *Communist Manifesto* and a year of tremendous significance for women's rights. In France, a second petition was introduced for women's suffrage (although legislative fraternity prevailed until 1944). And at a Friends' meeting house in upstate New York in 1848, the first women's conference convened, a conference considered to be the genesis of the women's movement on the international scale.

When we consider poetry by women in Russia, two distinct traditions emerge; first, is the tradition of *zhenskie stikhi* (woman's verse) *damskaya poezia* (ladies' poetry), the genteel craft of the poetess of the first half of the nineteenth century (who, unlike many of her English or American counterparts, is distinguished by her versatility in foreign languages and literary traditions). Then there is the tradition of the professional woman poet, a tradition that emerges strongly in the twentieth century; nor was it absent in the nineteenth century, though prose brought in most of the honoraria.

The impressive number of women writers in the relatively recent genesis of Russian literature has made our selection for this anthology quite difficult—it is by no means intended to represent all of the women writers. We chose to begin with Pavlova, the first to transcend "woman's verse" and representative of the two traditions. While the poetesses hold a significant place in the history of the woman writer in Russian literature, their works lend no support to any feminist argument for revising the traditional canon. We have included Rostopchina to demonstrate that women are capable of writing mediocre poetry and because she exemplifies the Bluestocking sensibility and presents the contemporary scholar with the challenge of dealing with woman's verse. We have given a disproportionately long summary of her biography to stress the normative character of her activities.

For the twentieth century, we have concentrated heavily on Akhmatova, Tsvetaeva, and Gippius, not only because their works mark the beginning of women's significant contribution to poetry and they are the first women poets of undisputed genius, but because they also mark a literary era. However, many of their contemporaries were also accomplished and well-known at the time: Elena Guro, both as a painter and poet, and the emigré Nina Bérberova. We have included Parnok because of her contemporary fame, and because her poetry speaks specifically to a celebration of womanhood. The impressive number of women poets speaks to the multivalences of the lyric voice and suggests Akhmatova's remark, "I taught women to speak/But God, how can they be stilled?" In-

4

deed, since the collapse of the Soviet Union, there are now groups of women writers, including "The Amazon," and even a feminist consciousness-raising group comprised of women writers from different professions. Given the number of women writers from 1925 to the present (Irina Ratushinskaya in exile, and Bella Akhmadulina, to name just two), an anthology including contemporary women would be extensive and exhaustive.

II: The Emergence of the Russian Poetess

Briusov kept saying "Woman. Passion. Love" into the twentieth century. But earlier, in 1837, the minor novelist Verevkin (pseudonym Rachmanyi) had written:

> Woman, dancing on a rope, woman lifting weights, woman-amazon, woman, playing the violin, woman, chewing tobacco before she's 35 years old, woman, beating her husband, finally, the woman-writer . . . Having aroused curiosity at first, she then engages in activity of profound repugnance. And it is natural. In these women there is no essence . . . Is it possible that they can with their small, fiery, naughty little heads refute the theory of electricity; compute the squaring of a circle; give lectures on botany, on the study of the skull, and federal finance, or become corrupted, composing novels of manners.[10]

And earlier still, in 1816, Dennis Davydov, the poet-partisan and contemporary of Pushkin, described "The Poetic Woman" as "a rush, confusion/Both coldness and delight,/Both refinery and enthusiasm, Laughter and tears, devil and god,/The sultriness of noon-day summer,/A hurricane's beauty,/A frenzied poet's Restless dream!/ With her friendship is rapture/But save us, creator, from/Love's relation with her,/And mysterious ties! /She is fiery, glory-loving,/I avow, that she is unshakeable, jealous/Like a legal wife!"[11] In 1826, Ivan Kireevsky admonished: "ladies of the wonderful sex, do not touch the Parnassian pen!" and reminded "comely bold lasses" that Amor had given them other gifts. He went on to note in 1834 "the very word authoress for a long time now perhaps was connected to the most unpleasant understandings: fingers in ink, pedantry in the mind, and typography in the heart!"[12] The spectre of a woman entering the literary scene prompted this from Pushkin:

> Like painted lips without a smile,
> Without grammatical mistake
> I do not like Russian speech.

It may be, to my defeat
A generation of new beauties,
Having heeded the beseeching voice of journals,
Will school us in grammar,
Will bring poetry into practice
But I . . . What's it to me? I will remain true to antiquity.[13]

A new generation of women had arisen in the nineteenth century, which, however, would not change the immediate course of Russian literature. Unlike Western European countries, Russia had had no strong secular literary tradition before the eighteenth century when a woman ruled the empire. Catherine the Great (1729–96) was at the helm of the nation for thirty-four years ; the German-born empress corresponded with the leading figures of Europe, in particular Voltaire, Diderot, and Grimm; she was not only instrumental in bringing European culture to Russia, and in its subsequent influence upon Russian literature, but was also a prolific author of prose, plays, satires, and tales, in her native German, French, and also Russian. A woman, Princess Dashkov, was also president of the Russian Academy.

Nevertheless, at that time, women were most influential as anonymous peasant tellers of folktales or as well-known performers at the court, where several made names for themselves as singers or ballet dancers so prominently that they appear in Pushkin's *Eugene Onegin*. In an age when Russian folk culture was discovered by the aristocracy, women were part of the charm of the peasant panorama: as the scholar Nikolai Bannikov puts it, women were essential decorations of religious festivals and plays performed by serfs.[14] Thus was born the simple peasant girl, Karamzin's "poor Liza," through whom the aristocracy learned the radical idea that "even peasant girls know how to love." This fascination with the national folk tradition and language, especially on the stage since the 1780s, grew in the aftermath of the Napoleonic invasion of 1812.

Women, though mostly kept in the background as members of their social class, served as the keepers of the flame of Russian culture and language for the major writers at a time when the aristocracy, and therefore the poets, all spoke French or German. (This dichotomy became a theme of the nineteenth-century novels; the language of the court remained foreign until 1917.) Woman's role as spinner of tales is immortalized in Pushkin's portrayal of his nanny, Arina Rodionovna, whose grave in Leningrad is still a shrine for literary pilgrimage. Despite women's influential if anonymous role, it remained for male writers such as Pyotr Kireevsky, Koltsov, Lermontov, Krylov, Afanasiev, and Pushkin to bring folk poetry and the folktale into the literary domain.

While Bannikov suggests that women's role as performers and singers contributes to the genesis of the woman writer, the peasant is hardly the precursor for the poetess, who has already appeared on the scene, to the manner born and wed, as the reciting hostess to male genius. The wives of the writers Derzhavin and Khieraskov wrote poetry. Elizaveta Khieraskova may have published in the first literary almanac; she and her husband hosted what may have been the first literary and musical salon in the 1760s. So did Avdotia Glinka, the wife of the composer Fedor Glinka, and Ekaterina Alexanderovna Knyazhnina, whom Lomonosov described as "an intelligent lady," the wife of the dramatist Knyazhnin. Many composed and performed lyrics.

Evdokia Rostopchina wrote over forty songs; her lyrics appeared in song-books and were used by such renowned composers as Glinka, Liszt, Rubenstein, and later Tschaikovsky. The young Anna Bunina (1774–1829) surprised her family by going off to the capital, St. Petersburg, and remaining there to become a member of the literary salons. Her translations of Batteaux and Boileau won the attention of contemporary critics. A collection of her own poetry, *The Inexperienced Muse*, was published in 1809; in 1811, *Village Evenings*; and another three-part collection in 1819–1821. She won the praise of Derzhavin and Karamzin. Nadezhda Sergeevna Teplova (1814–1848), the daughter of a well-to-do merchant family, published her first poem when she was thirteen; she organized musical evenings, and together with her sister Seraphima wrote poetry that they themselves published. Vyazemsky found in Teplova a "woman's perception of life," and noted that "in woman's confessions there is a special wonder."[15] At the end of the 1820s she and her sister were published in the *Ladies' Journal* and in other almanacs and journals. A collection of her poetry, published in 1833, was mentioned in reviews by Belinsky and Kireevsky; and in 1838 another edition followed. Her contemporary, A. A. Volkova, also tried to enter the literary life at the turn of the century, as did the fifteen-year-old Elizaveta Shakova in 1837. Ladies, plume in hand, were active even in Kazan, where Alexandra Fuchs published a collection of poetry in 1834. She was the wife of a doctor and professor, with whom Pushkin stayed in 1833 while researching the Pugachev uprising.

Women, however, were not instrumental in bringing poetry down to earth from its Parnassian, male-dominated heights. It remained for Belinsky, Dobroliubov, and Chernyshevsky to advocate the moral and social imperatives of literature, (including women's rights), a position that culminated in the socialist realism of the Soviet era, whereby literature must serve the ideology and be politically correct but not too representative about day-to-day reality. Nor did women make any significant contribution to the recurring theme of the epoch, Russia's spiritual, social and literary destiny. Still, a number of women were aware of the woman question, first raised in the wake of the French Revolution, and then influenced by George Sand (1804–1876), whom D. S. Mirsky called the mother of Russian realism (Gogol being the father).[16] Later, Russia had her Brontes, in the persons of the three Khvoschinskaya sisters. While hundreds of women were publishing stories and novels, there was as yet none significant enough to merit critical attention a century later.

According to the scholar V. Uchenova, a "pleiad of women writers" emerged on the scene in the 1830s and 1840s, primarily writing society tales influenced by the romantic movement.[17] The most well-known, Elena Andreevna Gan, who published under the pseudonym Zinaida R-va, (1814–1842), was hailed by Belinsky as the best woman writer in an article on her works and contemporary women writers.[18] Many others met with critical acclaim. Belinsky described Maria Zhukova's (1804–1855) stories Self Sacrifice, and Dacha on Peterhof Road, as written in a wonderful style that "men rarely master."[19] Dobroliubov found "remarkable" Zhadovskaya's novel, On the Side of High Society, published in the Russian Herald. Her prose, "A Woman's Story" and "Woman Abandoned," was published in the Dostoevsky brothers' journal, Vremya, in 1861. Nadezhda Durova, whose four-volume collection of works was published in 1840, met with criticism that soon overcame trite remarks based on gender. Pushkin wrote of the "animated, original, wonderful style" of her Maiden Cavalryman. He furthered her reputation in his journal, The Contemporary. Belinsky remarked that it seemed as if Pushkin had handed over his prose pen to her.[20]

Women writers gave the society tale a new dimension. As Xenia Gasiorowska points out, they were the first to display, at best, a George Sandist self-consciousness—and, one might add, at worst, a self-pity for the plight of the aristocratic lady in indicting the superficial conventions of high society for woman's lot. In Zhukova's tale, Self-Sacrifice, with its shades of female martyrdom, the heroine is another poor Liza. This time she is promoted to governess, in love once again with someone above her station. Rostopchina's novel A Happy Woman, ends with the phrase "a happy woman, murdered by her own happiness." The heroine of Gan's Society's Judgment (Sud Sveta) calls the authoress "cruel" and the woman writer "an uninvited guest"; still she was "a strange phenomenon." Gan herself lamented: "Who knows better than I all that is unpleasant, cruel, unnatural in the situation of a woman, who stands, so to speak, on a pedestal and makes of herself the goal of people's gazes and gossiping."[21]

This group, however, did more to advance the democratic critics' social agenda than to further woman's achievements in the literary arena. Belinsky's initial assessment was that the female temperament precluded the artistic process: "A woman must love the arts, but love them for pleasure, and not in order to become an artist herself. No, never can a woman-author not love, not be a wife and mother." Yet this most influential critic soon revised his opinion:

> The appellation of woman writer is still contraband at this time, not only in our [country] . . . Hardly does someone miss the chance, speaking of the woman writing, to mock the limitation of the female mind, as if it is more fit for the kitchen, the nursery, for sewing and knitting, than for thought and creativity . . . No sooner does the law leave woman in peace, then the opinion of society acts against her. A thousand-headed monster declares her immoral and dissolute, sullies her noblest feelings, purest intentions and aspirations, most elevated thoughts,—sullies them with the dirt of its own commentaries; declares her a shapeless comet, a monstrous appearance, willfully broken-free from the sphere of her own gender, from the circle of responsibilities, in order to allay her bridled passions and enjoy a clamorous and scandalous reputation.[22]

In Russia, where no one had the right to vote, the question became a polemic issue in the exciting intellectual climate of the 1830s and 1840s, and it persisted. Belinsky, the earliest champion of the cause, evinced a laudable consciousness. He noted that a woman receives "an education worse than pathetic and worthless, worse than false and unessential, constrained hand and foot by the iron despotism of barbaric customs and proprieties, victims of another's unconditional power all of her life, before marriage the slaves of parents, after marriage, the things of husbands."[23]

The democratic call increased throughout the century, with the woman question an obvious part of the social critics' agenda. The *raznochintsy*, intellectual and upper-class women, were far different from the poetesses of the earlier generation. Akhmatova's mother, for instance, was once a member of the People's Will. A change had taken place since the cardboard feminist of Chernyshevsky's *What Is to be Done* (1861), who figured in Turgenev's *Fathers and Children*, (1862), or in Dostoevsky's *The Possessed*, (1871–72) where any woman with feminist attributes was in conflict with the feminine Biblical paradigm of the author's complex cosmos. In contrast, *Anna Karenina* (1875–77), though written less than a decade later, offers a probing psychological portrait of an intellectual and liberated woman, despite the constricting confines of Tolstoy's moral schema and authorial revenge.

Women also made a contribution to the revolutionary and feminist imperative; for example, Vera Nikolaevna Figner (1852–1942), a poetess and member of the People's Will who saw the revolutionary call realized, was one of the many women who took active roles in politics, or revolutionary activities.[24] She helped make the explosives that assassinated Alexander II and, after two decades in prison, she led an ultimately successful demonstration for women's suffrage to the tune of the *Marseillaise*, approved at the second meeting of the Constitutional Assembly.[25] In the hindsight of Soviet revisionism, the aristocratic wives of the Decembrists become the first freedom fighters. Maria Volkonskaya (1805–1863), a cousin of the poetess, who accompanied her husband into exile, was one of the heroines of Nekrasov's "Russian Women." She may have been the first woman writer to enter into the tradition of exile literature in her *Notes of Siberia*.

Belinsky, when he wrote of a woman writer's "sublime sacrament of suffering," contributed to the view of the Russian woman epitomized in the title of this anthology, and to the cultural idea of the strong woman in the matriarchal aspect of Russian culture. The idea of sufferance, with its Orthodox connotation, has a tragic resonance in the Soviet era. But there is a great variety in the lives of these women poets. Consider, for example, Nadezhda Durova (1783–1866), whose autobiographical *The Maiden Cavalryman* won the interest of contemporary critics. She herself successfully entered a man's world as soldier and writer. The daughter of a Hussar cavalry captain and estate owner in the Ukraine, a wife and a mother, Durova followed in her father's footsteps. In September 1806, she put on a Cossack's outfit and joined the army, serving in the Napoleonic Wars. In the course of her military career Durova was promoted from cornet to staff-captain of cavalry. She served as an adjutant to General Kutuzov. Wounded in battle, she survived several military campaigns and was awarded the Georgian Cross for bravery. [26]

Or Princess Zinaida Alexanderovna Volkonskaya (1792–1862).[27] This poetess par excellence was the hostess to a Russian and European literary galaxy allegedly unanimous in praising her talents: her Moscow salon was the talk of the town in the 1820s. Pushkin dedicated "Gypsies" to her and called her: "Queen of the Muses and of beauty,/You hold with your gentle hand/The magical scepter of inspiration,/And above the pensive brow,/Genius both hovers and glows."[28] Born in Italy to a prince who was serving as a minister there, she early displayed a gift for music and languages, and could recite Corneille and Dante, though she found Russian to be "une

10

lacune fâccheuse." She preferred the language of Voltaire to that of Pushkin and wrote primarily in French. As a member of the titled upper class the young princess was presented at court, serving as an attendant to the Queen of Prussia. Her husband, an aide-de-camp to the Tsar, was sent on a secret mission to Napoleon in 1808. The French Emperor, impressed by his diplomatic skills, asked the Russian emissary to convey to the Tsar that together they could hold the world in the palm of their hands. While the Princess was not engaged in diplomatic missions, she was friend and confidante to Tsar Alexander I. She composed a poem to music upon his death, with verses dedicated to the Empress. Volkonskaya also played a significant part in the intrigue following the Decembrist revolt. When her brother-in-law, Sergei Volkonsky, and her cousin's husband, Trubetskoi, were arrested, their wives decided to go with them to Siberia, and the princess achieved fame for her valedictory verses on these sad occasions. Though hardly a revolutionary, Volkonskaya was under the surveillance of the secret police and the Third Section, created by Nicholas I for civil order and investigations; she was considered dangerous, her salon viewed as the gathering place for subversive malcontents.

Volkonskaya was published in contemporary journals, where Madame de Stael found and admired her poem, "La Musique." Not content just to play the muse, Volkonskaya apparently founded a *lycée* in Odessa. Her talents extended beyond the reflective life of poetry, for she was also a musician, composer, and performer, winning plaudits as a singer in a private staging of a Rossini opera in Paris. Rossini himself admired her singing. She also wrote music for the opera "Joan of Arc." Bruni painted her, a portrait she later offered to Pushkin. Volkonskaya built her own theatre in her house on Tverskaya Street in Moscow (1824). She was also a talented and serious researcher of Russian and Scandinavian folklore, but published the results of her research anonymously. The historical novel, *Slavic Picture (Miliada: Tableau Slave du Vième siècle)* appeared first in French in 1824 and was well received; the Russian translation was prefaced with high praise by a professional (i. e., male) historian. After this, Volkonskaya became the first woman member of the Society of History and Antiquities at Moscow University. She may also be among the first Russian women writers to attempt an epic story in her *Tale of Olga,* a work based on the legendary princess. Excerpts of this unfinished historical tale were published in Moscow in 1836, as were her *Lettres d'Italie.* After her conversion to Roman Catholicism, Volkonskaya left Russia in 1829 for Italy, stopping en route to visit Goethe. She spent the rest of her long life in Italy, returning only twice to visit Russia. Her Italian villa became

11

a haven for Russian writers, including Gogol, and its garden was filled with statues of her Russian poet-friends.

Many of these women led enviable lives, with the exception of Pavlova, whose life was marked by a fall from fame and a downward mobility, thanks to a husband who gambled away her estate. Her rival, Rostopchina, however, owned estates in Italy and Russia; she would recite verses before young ladies, or compose poems while riding in her carriage between Moscow and her estate. This versifying conservative socialite exhibited a sense of *noblesse oblige,* a moral outrage at her class, a sympathy with the poor peasant in the huts, and a shallow bigotry. Unlike Pavlova, the countess did not die impoverished or unrecognized, but she did spend the last two years of her life in chronic illness, subjected to scathing attacks on her writing by utilitarian critics who called her a "recreant." A symbol of aristocratic craft, she was condemned as "demonic" and "evil" twenty-eight years after her death by Nekrasova, a critic from the socialist camp. The poet who adopted the pseudonym "Clear-Sighted Woman" never escaped Belinsky's label of her as "confined to the ball." Her view of women and writing, however, can be said to parody itself.

By contrast, Pavlova did enjoy considerable literary acclaim. Belinsky called her translations "diamonds," Goethe and Pushkin praised her poetry. Yet she was parodied by her adversary Ivan Panaev, and by the poet Nikolai Nekrasov, who as a radical disapproved even of male efforts in the spirit of Pavlova's poetry; he was strongly supportive of progressive women writers; he used the example of Pavlova to lament that women renounced the achievements of the culinary arts, jelly and pickles for poetry. An anonymous article that praised her poetry as original, remarkable, but hardly feminine went on to laud the poet for raising the women's question in her novel. But then the critic lamented that young girls and women now lacked "the desire to please," to change from svelte brides to full-bodied wives.[29] Rostopchina called her a Bluestocking and mocked her knowledge of many languages. Hardly accused of writing sentimental, ladies' verse, she was criticized by the utilitarian camp of writing poetry that was distant from real life. Even to her friend, the Slavophile Ivan Aksakov, Pavlova was "a curious psychological subject," worthy of study because she appeared unshaken by catastrophe: the loss of her name and social position, the separation from her son, and the need to work for a living. Instead of praising her triumph over adversity, this critic accused her of "loving no one," of holding nothing sacred, and merely using her experience for her art, deriding her dedication to her craft and the "external exaltation" that it gave her.[30]

12

Nor did the confident, "majestic, rhetorical" air that Pavlova adapted when reading her poetry suit the image of the poetess, and she incurred considerable ridicule.[31] Although she, like many male romantic epigones in an antiromantic age, was criticized for her abstract verse of a bygone era, the successful, confident Pavlova also exemplifies what Suzanne Juhasz calls the double bind for a woman poet, the conflict between a lyric poet's self-assertion and a woman's diffidence. As Barbara Heldt points out, the specter of the woman-poet , reading her poetry as was the fashion, was ridiculed; "In this way was engendered a more subtle conflict than that of poet versus society—that of woman-poet versus society, and ultimately, of woman versus poet—within Pavlova herself."[32] The confident Pavlova also felt that feminine vanity took precedence over authorial egotism, as the poet wrote to her friend Panaev: "I do not repudiate my sex and have not conquered its weaknesses; whatever you may say, a woman-poet always remains more woman than poet and authorial egotism in her is weaker than female egotism. . . . I have never wished nor tried to make myself an author; this necessity that exists in me for better or for worse, this calling I keep in check as much as I can..."(Heldt's transl.)[33]

Pavlova displays an ambivalence toward her sex, disdaining female verse while seeking other female voices. In "Reading the poems of a young girl," for example, she makes fun of ladies' verse; in "We are contemporaries, Countess" she mocks Rostopchina as a George Sandist. In the Dedication of A Double Life, Pavlova searches for other women writers, and in "Three Souls," she portrays herself and two other female poets as divinely ordained for the vocation. One of these, a martyr to the female poet's cause, is an American named Lucretia Maria Davidson (1808–25), who died at age seventeen, strangely finding her way into an article in a Russian journal of 1830 (Literaturnaya Gazeta).[34]

In A Double Life. Pavlova is the first Russian woman writer to articulate the poet's double bind on a complex psychological level. This novel is partly a satirical indictment of the moral code and values of the beau monde, focused on women. Written in an unconventional and original form, A Double Life combines a society tale with sequences of lyric poetry that reflect the heroine's dreams. Its style transcends the work of more self-pitying and self-conscious Sandist novelists. The protagonist, Cecily, is a feminist's anti-heroine, the novel an antithesis of Kate Chopin's The Awakening, but it still offers only glimmerings of a nascent consciousness, of the struggles of female creativity and sexuality against repression. For Cecily, as for other socialites, poetry and the arts serve not as enrichments for her mind but as accoutrements to get her beau. As a tale of manners the novel provides a window into the drawing room of nineteenth-century Russia, with fast-paced dialogue and debates on art and women's education. Its confines are juxtaposed to the inner freedom afforded by her own room; once again, the topos of the room is emblematic of a female psychology and of an interior freedom and source of creativity. When she is alone Cecily has dreams of poetry, with a male muse, but she does not yield to the inner voice. Instead she bears the conjugal crown. Since she is unaware of her vocation, she is not even capable of sacrifice. Here is no Tolstoyan blush of feminine ignorance-as-bliss, no sign of woman's natural, intuitive superiority. Nor is there any Cassandra pose of the female poet who has the gift of prophecy but is not believed. The novel ends on an ambiguous note that affirms Cecily's dormant consciousness.

In "Quadrille," [35] Pavlova also addresses the theme of woman's destiny and identity. Here the countess remarks: "Sensible consideration was hindered by/Both the eternal bane of adulation/And cherished whim of meditation;/And the incoherence of a woman's role;/ A mixture of self-will and captivity/Is almost always our destiny. / Where in the labyrinth of upbringing/Is the guiding string?" Pavlova was the first to lend coherence and depth to such questions.

III: The Professional Woman Poet of the 20th Century

The derogatory limitations implied by the role of the poetess were still very much in force at the turn of the century. If Pavlova was the first to endure considerable censure for being a woman writer, those who followed also faced some of the scandal also associated with the remote art of a bygone era. Akhmatova's father had teased her as a child by calling her "a decadent poetess." When she decided to publish, she changed her name so as not to sully his. But in 1909 Annensky attempted to better the climate by devoting an article to the subject in *Apollon*, and in 1914, Ivanov-Razumnik called for a serious study of the poetess's art in his "Affected Creatures: Akhmatova's *Rosary* and Vera Inber's *Sorrowful Wine*" (*Zavety*, No. 5). Yet Mayakovsky called the plethora of ladies' names in publications, "chirpings."[36] Even Mandelshtam—though he had written of Akhmatova's poetry in 1916 as "fast approaching the point of becoming one of the symbols of the greatness of Russia"[37] and exempted her from his critique—uses the pejorative negative resonances of *damskaya stikhi* to exemplify bad poetry, whether written by men or women, in 1922;

... Women's poetry is the worst aspect of literary Moscow ... The majority of Moscow poetesses have been injured by metaphor. These are the poor Isises doomed to the eternal quest after the second half of a poetic simile which was lost somewhere, and which is obliged to return its primal unity to the poetic image to Osiris ... Adalis and Marina Tsvetaeva are prophets, as is Sofia Parnok. Their prophecy is a kind of domestic needlework. While the elevated tone and intolerable bombastic rhetoric of men's poetry has subsided, yielding to a more normal use of the vocal apparatus, feminine poetry continues to vibrate at the highest pitch, offending the ear, offending the historical, poetical sense.

(translated by Jane Gary Harris
and Constance Link)[38]

Severianin called Akhmatova's poetry "a slander" to women[39]; his remarks, like Mayakovsky's, are particularly informed by the machismo strain of Futurism. And as late as 1940, she still received "Dear Anna Andreevna" letters from women thanking her for writing about the tribulations of love and of men's deception.[40] Yet graver were the politically motivated attacks. According to revolutionary ideology, which made a point of ignoring gender and sex, women poets were denounced as vestiges of a bourgeois consciousness. In *Literature and Revolution* (1923), Trotsky felt it important enough to take time from restructuring society to turn his attention to anthologies of women's poetry. He singled out Akhmatova and Tsvetaeva, among others, for their religiosity; he accused them of having a "small lyric circle" with a God who, "quite housebroken," sometimes performs "the duties of a doctor to feminine complaints."(Trans. by Sam Driver)[41] In *On Guard,* Tsvetaeva's use of traditional Moscow themes was viewed by the critic Rodov as showing "the cult of the Virgin and of the church." (Trans. Simon Karlinsky). Mayakovsky joined in the calumny, calling her poetry "gypsy lyrics" in 1926.[42]

Akhmatova, the former wife of the poet and former officer in the Tsar's Army, Nikolai Gumilev (executed in 1921), became the center of the debates of the Party critics and the Formalists alike. The Formalist Eikhenbaum's earlier description of the poet as "part nun, part harlot" was meant to describe a positive attribute of her lyric persona, but it was used in 1923 by the Left Art critic Arvatov, in a polemic with Alexandra Kollontai, whose theories about open-love were also attacked in "Madame Akhmatova and Comrade Kolontai,"in *Molodaya Gvardia*.[43] (Kollontai had been the People's

Commissar of Social Welfare after the Revolution, the head of the Worker's Opposition. Later, after she accepted the Stalinist line, she became Ambassador to Sweden.) This infamous label was ultimately used by Zhdanov, in charge of the purges in Leningrad, who in 1946 launched a vilifying campaign against Akhmatova and the immensely popular writer, Zoshchenko, that ruined their lives.

The poet who had formerly been viewed as "bourgeois" gave a radio address during the War that praised the strength and courage of Leningrad's women. She published a poem in *Pravda* on International Woman's Day, 1942. In 1945 she was named the best of the Leningrad poets by the journals *Zvezda* and *Leningrad*. Yet after Zhdanov's campaign, her poetry was considered "trash." Even those who had never heard of Akhmatova soon recognized her name, and Zoshchenko's, through the many articles and lectures where they were used as examples of anti-Sovietism. Akhmatova was expelled from the Writer's Union and her son was arrested for the third time in 1949, and only released in 1956.

Akhmatova never recanted, no matter how this would have eased her life; as Sam Driver puts it, she never compromised her artistic integrity or personal dignity. Driver discusses the "moral essence" of her poetry in relation to her aesthetic and in the context of Akhmatova's comments on Mandelshtam, and his remarks while in exile in Voronezh in 1937, and his definition of acmeism as "A longing for world culture." As Driver comments, such seemingly harmless remarks, later transformed and associated with dangerous "subservience to the West" or "cosmopolitanism" in the Stalinist era, were brave statements. Driver cites Mandelshtam's earlier definition (1922) that "Acmeism is not only a literary but also a social phenomenon in Russian history. With [Acmeism] in Russian poetry, moral strength was reborn." He then comments:

> Significantly, in Mandelshtam's article, true morality is identified with courage—the courage to stand for the right whatever the danger. It is in this light that Akhmatova's bold and unadumbrated quotation from Mandelshtam—"*Ia ne otrekaius' ni ot zhivykh ni ot mertvykh*"["I forswear neither the living nor the dead"]—begins to take on a much broader meaning, one which is consonant with Akhmatova's own idea of higher morality: the courage to stand for the right in the most Christian sense of concern for one's brother, one's fellow man, *l'autrui, blizhnii*. Certainly this particular virtue is a gentle and most unexceptionable one in other times, in other places, but in the nightmare world in which Akhmatova

lived most of her adult life, her moral stand meant a trial by fire and almost unbearable suffering.[44]

In *Requiem*, Akhmatova dared to voice the moral imperative of remembrance through poetry; here the lyric persona of one woman encompassed the universality of Russia's sufferance during the Terror.

Both Akhmatova and Tsvetaeva attest to the prominent role of the poet in Russian culture. Akhmatova remained a powerful figure during her long silence. Tsvetaeva was censored and condemned in the Literary Encyclopedia of 1934, years after she had left the Soviet Union.

IV. The 'Woman's Question' in Poetry

In the poets selected for this anthology there is rich material for feminist analysis. Tsvetaeva's powerful range of voice, and her presentation of mythic figures like the amazon, or Sybill, provoke compelling and complex questions about the feminine. Her poetry, as well as that of Gippius, and other women represented here, raise significant questions and speak to the multivalences of the lyric voice, particularly in its differences, in a language that is largely gender-defined. For example, Tsvetaeva's poems may be unmarked for gender, (in particular the poem "On a Red Steed" has a male muse), whereas Akhmatova's are primarily marked. One might argue that Tsvetaeva, even in her early "Evening Album," validates what is usually considered a woman's pejorative, domestic discourse, and elsewhere affirms motherhood in her many poems to her children.

The Russian woman poet of the 20th century continues the tradition of *grazhdanskie stikhi* (civic verse), certainly beginning with the 1860s, and unlike the stereotypes of her Western counterparts, is never in a marginal position to public events. Compare, for example, Emily Dickinson, Higginson's "eccentric poetess," always presented as distant and disinterested in history; this stereotype of the Anglo-American woman poet arguably originated with Elizabeth Barrett Browning who, though she also wrote civic verse, including a letter to Napoleon on behalf of Victor Hugo, is viewed primarily as a frail bluestocking. Tsvetaeva's final cycle, *Poems to Czechoslovakia*, is a complex orchestration of lyrics, voiced in outrage at the betrayal by her beloved Germany of the "homeland of her son," and one of the most powerful diatribes of the events that precipitated World War II. In her early cycle "The Demesne of the Swans," she is at once wife, mother, witness to civil war, and "the chronicler" of the White Army with "a soldier's stance." Gippius also wrote anti-Bolshevik poems. Akhmatova articulates woman's heroism and sufferance; yet her stance is tied to the traditional role of the Russian poet, "to whom it is not given to die a bright death." Any attempt at analysis must take into account the complex intricacies of Russian culture and the paradoxical terrain of poetry. Analogies to Western writers underscore the differences. H. D., for instance, resembles Akhmatova as an imagist, and in her association with major writers and figures of the age: D. H. Lawrence, Pound, Eliot, and later Freud; yet, one cannot imagine her being considered for the Nobel Prize or awarded an honorary degree by Oxford.

If one looks for analogies, oddly enough, Tsvetaeva and Emily Dickinson share certain aspects in their poetics. While Dickinson does not have a diversified range of works, both exhibit ellipsis, privileged solitude (uedinenie), and a seclusion in the other life of poetry, what Dickinson called "finite infinity." Both are highly philosophical poets who can be seen as redefining their native traditions as no one else has. Yet they arrive at a common ground by two divergent avenues in two distinct cultures: Dickinson, whatever the state of her psyche, wrote out of a "polar privacy"; and though she was the daughter of a senator, who wrote most of her poetry during the American Civil War, civic themes are curiously absent from it. Tsvetaeva, by contrast, is the public and daring woman, without the freedom Dickinson found in a "turn of the key" to her room. Tsvetaeva's life in emigration exemplifies not only the hardships of an émigré writer in exile, but the very real domestic constraints and drudgery of a woman's historic place; her poetry conveys the drudgery ("Life's Train," for example, with the clutter of diapers, and harsh sybillants suggest a woman's entrapment in a dialectic against the other life); yet her triumph through poetry renders Virginia Woolf's lament for "A Room of One's Own" a tempest in a Bloomsbury teacup.

Although Tsvetaeva asserted that there is no woman's question in relation to art in the epigraph to her essay, she goes on to approve of it in its military resolution,"the legendary reigns of Penthesileia [amazon queen], Brunhilde, Maria Morevna,"—in the Petrograd woman's battalion, as well as in schools for seamstresses. The passage concludes with:

> . . . there are woman's responses to the human question, such as: Sappho, Joan of Arc, St. Teresa, Bettina Brentano. There are enchanting woman's wailings (Lettres de Mademoiselle de Lespinasse), there is a woman's idea (Maria Bashkirtseva), there is a woman's paintbrush (Rosa Bonheur), but all of this—is set apart from the woman's question, and

by its lack of suspicion in relation to it, has destroyed and annihilated it.

In their very different responses, Marina Tsvetaeva and Anna Akhmatova raise the basic questions that are the domain of poetry. In doing so, these two of the greatest poets of this century redefine the protean nature of women's verse, challenging us to rephrase the questions about the interrelations of gender and literary perception.

Tsvetaeva once put her acclaim in the future perfective. Banned for decades, she is now attaining wide readership in the former Soviet Union, with an official sanction that no one could have anticipated a few years ago. An Akhmatova museum opened in Leningrad in 1990, and the Tsvetaeva museum has opened in August 1992 in Moscow in the house where the poet once lived. In the summer of 1989, a chance viewing of late night TV in the Hotel Ukraine in Moscow, one of the seven Stalinist edifices, showed a performance of "Requiem," with a woman dressed like Akhmatova and a chorus of soldiers. The cynic might say that this image exemplifies *glasnost*, its looking-glass reality, or else was its price at a time when dialogue about the 1917 February Revolution had renewed with increasing intensity prior to the recent dissolution of the Soviet Union. One hopes it also marks a turn where, in the words of Akhmatova, the poet once condemned as a pernicious influence on Soviet youth: "Out of such ruins do I speak!/ Out of such devastation do I cry out! . . . And nevertheless they shall recognize my voice./ And nevertheless they shall once again believe it."

Notes

[1]Marina Tsvetaeva, "Geroi Truda (zapisi o Valerii Briusove)," *Izbrannaia proza v dvukh tomakh, 1917–1937,* ed. Alexander Sumerkin, Preface by Joseph Brodsky, (New York: Russica, 1979) Vol. 1: 197.

[2]Marina Zvétaieva, *Mon frére féminin : lettre à l'Amazone* (Paris: Mercure de France, 1979) 11. "Amazone" is the American expatriate, Natalie Barney, friend of Cocteau, Proust, Pound, Eliot, among many others, who proclaimed her lesbianism under this title, and was the addressee of Rémy de Gourmont's widely known collection *Lettres à l'Amazone.*

[3]I am borrowing the term from Suzanne Juhasz: *Naked and Fiery Forms: Modern American Poetry by Women: A New Tradition* (New York: Harper Colophon Books, 1976), quoted in Sandra M. Gilbert and Susan Gubar, *The Madwoman in the Attic: The Woman Writer and the Nineteenth Century Literary Imagination* (New Haven: Yale UP 1979) 584.

[4]Lydia Chukovskaya, *Zapiski ob Anne Akhmatovoi* , (Paris: YMCA Press, 1976), Vol. 1:70.

[5]In her book *On Chinese Women*, Kristeva transforms the daring, outspoken Tsvetaeva into a suicidal shade named Maria, whose prolific range of works is ignored, to demonstrate an impulse to the language of the feminine echolalic, and to show, as she argues in the beginning of her text, that "questions about woman's awakening" "show that woman *as such* does not exist." (her italics.) (p. 16). Kristeva, a Marxist and psychoanalyst, renders Tsvetaeva as "disillusioned with the revolution," when she was against it from the start. The only poem quoted in this essay, "I who want not to be" is Sylvia Plath's Julia Kristeva, *On Chinese Women*, trans. Anita Barrows (New York: Urizen, 1977).

[6]Some others were: Alexandra Exter (1882–1949), Elena Guro (1877–1913), Ksenia Ender (1895–1955), Maria Ender (1897–1942), Vera Pestel (1886–1952), Olga Rozanova (1886–1918), Antonina Sofronova (1892–1966), Varvara Stepanova (1894-1958), Nadezhda Udaltsova (1886–1961).

On the Russian Avant-Garde, See: *Russian Avant-Garde Art: The George Costakis Collection*, gen. ed. Angelica Zander Rubenstine, Intro. by S. Frederick Starr, (New York: Abrams 1981)

John E. Bowlt, ed. and trans., *Russian Art of the Avant-garde: Theory and Criticism 1902–1934* (New York: Viking, 1976)

Camilla Gray, *The Russian Experiment in Art: 1863–1922*, (New York: Thames and Hudson 1962, 1986).

Robert C. Williams, *Artists in Revolution: Portraits of the Russian Avant-garde, 1905–1925.* (Bloomington: Indiana UP, 1977).

[7]*Moscow Women, Thirteen Interviews by Carola Hansson and Karin Liden, trans. by Gerry Bothmer, George Blecher, and Lone Blecher,* intro. by Warshofsky Lapidus (New York: Pantheon Books, Random House,1983) xiv.

[8]Xenia Gasiorowska, "Women and Russian Literature," *Handbook of Russian Literature,* ed. Victor Terras, (New Haven: Yale UP 1983) 519–522.

[9]Barbara Heldt, intro. to her *A Double Life* by Karolina Pavlova (Oakland; Barbary Coast, 1986).

[10]V. V. Uchenova, intro. *Dacha na Petergofskoi doroge: Proza russkikh pisatel'nits pervoi polovinoi XIX veka* (Moscow: Sovremennik, 1986) 3–4.

On the nineteenth century woman writer, I am primarily following Uchenova.

[11]Dennis Vasilievich Davydov, "Poeticheskaya Zhenschinas": *Poety Pushkinskoi Pory,* ed. N.N. Bannikov (Moscow: Moskovskii Rabochii, 1981) 69–70.

Dennis Vasilievich Davydov was a contemporary of Pushkin; he described himself as "partisan not poet" ("Cossack.") He was known for his distinguished military career throughout Europe. Sir

Walter Scott had a portrait of him in his office. Although Davydov mocked the "Poetic Woman," Rostopchina wrote a tribute to him.

[12]Nikolai Bannikov, intro. *Russkie Poetessy XIX Veka*, (Moscow: Sovetskaya Rossiya, 1979) 9, 8.

[13]Uchenova 4.

[14]Bannikov, *Russkia Poetessy*.

[15]Bannikov, *Russkia Poetessy* 10.

[16]S. Mirsky, *A History of Russian Literature*, 1926 (Reprint, New York:Vintage Paperbacks) 178

[17]Uchenova.

[18]Uchenova 456. Gan was the daughter of Princess Dolgorukaya, and the mother of the theosophist Elena Blavatsky.

[19]Uchenova 458.

[20]Uchenova 7.

[21]Gan, Uchenova, 153, 6.

[22]Belinsky, Uchenova 4–9.

[23]Uchenova 5.

[24]Francine du Plessix Gray, *Soviet Women: Walking the Tightrope* (New York: Doubleday, 1990) 92–93.

[25]Uchenova 13.

[26]An interesting comparative analysis would be with a woman American novelist, Deborah Sampson, (1760–1827), of Massachusetts, who also donned a uniform and served in the Continental Army for two years.

Durova's work is available in an English translation:

Mary Fleming Zirin, trans. and ed., *The Cavalry Maiden: Journals of a Female Russian Officer in the Napoleonic Wars,* (London: Angel, 1988)

[27]Information on Volkonskaya's biography is from:

1. Hermione de Poltoratzky, *Profils russes. Une princesse russe à Rome, La Comtesse Roumiantzeff, Un évêque russe, Marfa Possadnitza*, (Paris: Perrin et Cie,1913).

2. M. Azadovsky, "Iz materialov 'Stroganovskoi Akademii': Neopublikovannye proizvedeniia Ksav'e de Mestra i Zinaidy Volkonskoi." *Literaturnoe Nasledstvo*, 33–34 (1939) 195–214.

3. Uchenova 3–4.

4. Bannikov 198

[28]Uchenova 6.

[29]Pavel Gromov, intro. *Polnoe Sobranie Stikhotvorenii*, by Karolina Pavlova, ed. N. M. Gaidenkov, (Moscow-Leningrad: Sovetskii Pisatel', 1964).

[30]Heldt viii.

[31]Heldt.

[32]Heldt ii.

[33]Heldt x.

[34]Gaidankov 557.

[35]"Quadrille" is a conversation in verse, a form frequently used by
Pavlova; the fast-paced tempo and shift in voice and dialect
underscore the title's metaphor. As Gromov points out, the central
question raised but not resolved is the talk of the town: whether
society or woman is responsible for her position. It is in part the
next chapter to A Double Life; but unlike the novel's young
debutantes, these women tell their own story, and have already
crossed "the decisive threshold" of marriage and independence and
are disillusioned if not bitter with real life and the loss of the ideals
of their girlhood. (Gromov, 44-45) Each comes from a different
background, and speaks in a different manner. There is yet
another poor Liza, who lives with her cruel and sickly aunt in a
remote village; her aunt's final bequest, however, is not enough for
Liza's suitor. Her story won the praises of the more utilitarian
critics. Parallels are also drawn to Eugene Onegin.

[36]Dmitri Khrenkov, Anna Akhmatova: V Peterburge - Petrograde -
Leningrade, (Leningrad: Lenizdat, 1989) 53–54.

[37]Chukovskaya 92.

[38]Osip Mandelshtam, The Complete Critical Prose and Letters, ed. Jane
G. Harris, trans. J. G. Harris and Constance Link, (Ann Arbor:
Ardis, 1979) 146.

[39]Chukovskaya 133.

[40]Chukovskaya 145.

[41]Sam Driver, Anna Akhmatova (New York:Twayne's World Authors
Series 198, 1972) 93.

[42]Simon Karlinsky, Marina Tsvetaeva: The Woman, Her World and her
Poetry (New York: Cambridge UP, 1985) 130, 131.

On the attacks on Tsvetaeva, Karlinsky writes: "It is indeed
striking that in their desire to discredit Tsvetaeva's poetry for
personal (Mandelshtam) or political (Trotsky and Mayakovsky)
reasons, these three famous men chose to attack it not as poetry
but as something written by a woman and for that reason inferior.
We can only speculate whether this approach, unlikely in either
pre-revolutionary or émigré criticism, was connected in any way
with the 1922–3 campaign in the Soviet press to discredit feminist
concerns as irrelevant to the new communist society. The campaign, aimed at the theories of Alexandra Kollontai and Anna
Akhmatova's poetry, was instigated by Lenin's wife, Nadezhda
Krupskaya, with her husband's full approval. " (131)

[43]Driver, Anna Akhmatova

[44]Sam Driver, "Anna Akhmatova: Theory and Practice," Canadian-
American Slavic Studies: 22, Nos. 1–4 (1988) 347.

Karolina Pavlova
(1807–1893)

For you the giving of this thought,
The greeting of my poetry,
For you this work of solitude,
Slaves of din and vanities.
All of you, unmet Cecilies,
My sorrowful breath has named in quietude,
All of you Psyches deprived of wings,
Mute sisters of my soul!
May God grant you too, unknown family,
Amid the sinful lie just one sacred dream,
In the captivity of this closed life
Just a momentary surge of that other life.

("Dedication," *A Double Life*)

In a life that spanned almost the entire nineteenth century, Karolina Pavlova epitomizes the double bind of the woman poet and the exile. In Moscow, where her talent was recognized early, she became a hostess to the aristocracy and to male genius, a controversial figure in an era charged with intellectual debate, and a frequent subject of scandal. In Germany, where she spent almost half her life, her aesthetic of the dominant inner chord in poetry was strengthened by the stresses of exile and the challenge of economic hardship and social censure.

Pavlova led the double life of a woman within the company of the greatest writers of her era, and within the woman's interiors of the drawing room, where she was an outsider by virtue of her writer's consciousness. She was fascinated by genius, especially poetic genius, and she was as unconventional in her attempt to be considered an equal to men in her private life as she was in her work, from her early life within writers' circles to her later relationship with a much younger man. [1]

The poet was born Karolina Jaenisch in Yaroslavl, the daughter of a Moscow professor and doctor who preferred to teach because he could not stand the thought of being responsible for someone's death. Pavlova's mother was of English and French descent; her father's family were long-time German residents of Moscow. She was tutored at home since there were as yet no schools of higher education for girls in Moscow and her biography evinces the superlative training in foreign languages and literary traditions that young ladies of the privileged class could obtain.

Through the princess and poetess Volkonskaya, Pavlova met the leading luminaries of the age, including Pushkin, Delvig, Vyazemsky, and the master of society tales, Odoevsky. Here, she was also introduced to the great Polish poet Mickiewicz, who became her Polish tutor, and then offered her "his hand and heart." Pavlova had been named the heiress to an uncle's estate, and she feared jeopardizing the potential bequest. Although her father was willing to make the sacrifice, Pavlova "followed the voice of duty" and rejected Mickiewicz. After an absence from Moscow of ten months, the poet offered her his friendship instead, and this romance had a lasting influence. Mickiewicz was the major love of her life; years later she wrote: "He's mine, as he was once." [2]

In 1836, she married Nikolai F. Pavlov, a well-known writer, who had been born a serf, and was a university graduate. His first stories had won Pushkin's praise,[3] and were also among the first to attack serfdom. For a time (1839-1844), the Pavlov household became the leading literary salon in Moscow; the guest-list included Turgenev, Gogol, Herzen, and Fet. Marriage, however, proved to be Pavlova's financial and social nemesis. Unlike Mary Wollstonecraft Shelley or Elizabeth Barrett Browning, who were overshadowed by their husbands, Pavlova's acclaim exceeded that of her husband, a success that he apparently resented as his own reputation declined. Pavlov admitted that his only deceptive act (*gadost'*) was that he had engaged in an ordinary calculation by marrying for money. Pavlov used his wife's estate for his gambling debts, mortgaged it without her knowledge, and took up with her cousin, whom she had befriended and welcomed into their home. After bankrupting her estate, he established another household with his wife's once poorer relation.

The proverbial double standard applies to the way Pavlova was treated by her contemporaries, some of whom went so far as to parody her in writing. When she took legal action against her husband for bankrupting her, a search of his library revealed prohibited books and he was arrested and sent into exile in Perm for ten months. Pavlov, the manumitted serf and fighter against serfdom, had the liberals on his side. His wife by then had won the sympathy of the Slavophiles though she did not take sides in the debate. Although Pavlova had not anticipated his arrest, their friends blamed her and did not forgive her. She was once again the cause of social censure when her father died of cholera and she left Saint Petersburg before the burial for fear of contracting the disease. In 1853, Pavlova left Russia with her son and mother for Dorpat in Livonia, and in 1857, for Germany. A few years after her move to Germany, she described her situation as hopeless, remarking in a letter to a friend in Russia: "I want to see whether everything that befalls me will strengthen me; whether I will withstand it or not." Although she was not entirely without supporters and friends, such as the writer Aleksei Tolstoi,[4] she died impoverished and forgotten.

In Pavlova's initial career she was at the center of a galaxy of international talent that included Pushkin and Goethe, who wrote poems to her in her album and praised her work. She published her first collection of translations and original poems in German (*Das Nordlicht,* 1833). As a gifted translator, Pavlova earned the praise of the leading critic, Belinsky, who commented on her unusual talent, her powerful energy, and the simplicity of her "diamond translations" into Russian.[5] Pavlova wrote poetry in German and French; she also knew Italian, Spanish, Swedish, and Dutch. Thanks in part to her, Russian literature was discovered in Europe and its reputation established. Her collection *Preludes* (Paris, 1839), containing her version of Schiller's *Jeanne d'Arc* and original French poems, won the interest of Balzac. She also translated a diverse range of authors in several genres from English, French, German, Polish, and even classical Greek. [6]

Although the woman question informs a substantial part of Pavlova's opus, her work is not limited to it and further reflects a distance from "ladies' verse." She wrote civic poetry and meditations on the philosophy of history, Russia's destiny, which suggest the Slavophile point of view. Themes of the homeland and nostalgia abroad, of Moscow versus St. Petersburg, also figure in her poetry, as do civic calls for freedom.[7] Pavlova's poetry contains the mark of a greater poet than her contemporary female rivals, a scope of vision on political or social themes that accommodates contradiction, often with wit and irony. Her poetry offers a perspective that finds categorical definition limiting; it points to the fallibility of the human condition, be it a view of the "lawless communist" versus the priggish Christian, or an expressed uneasiness when faced with the idea of the progress of civilization.[8]

As Barbara Heldt points out, Pavlova was the first Russian woman poet to devote her life to what she called her "sacred craft," and the first to achieve her aim of being taken seriously as a writer. She is not just the best of the nineteenth-century poetesses, most of whose works lend no support to any question of revising the traditional canon to include them. While Rostopchina and Volkonskaya extended the repertoire of ladies' verse, Pavlova disbarred the derogatory implication in the term "poetess." By her dedication to her craft and aesthetic, Pavlova epitomizes "that other life" of poetry that Emily Dickinson called her "guest of solitude."[9] Pavlova's novel *A Double*

Life begins with Byron, a great influence on all Russian poets of the time. Both Dickinson and Pavlova emphasize the romantic lyric poet's sense of solitude (*uedinenie*), an isolation that could be conceived of as enhanced by the fact of gender.

Central to Pavlova's work is the romantic view of the poet as "an unneeded guest in this world, an unknown nightingale" ("The Poet"), indignant at the sacrifice of the Muse at the marketplace ("Laeterna Magica"). Much of it involves philosophical meditation. She was criticized by the utilitarian critics then dominant for writing abstract poetry and for stressing "beautiful sounds" more than content, qualities aimed at in symbolist aesthetic decades later. Finally Pavlova's work won the attention of Briusov, who issued a collection of her poetry in 1915. But like other epigones of Pushkin (Aleksei Tolstoy, Maikov, Lev Mai, Polonsky), Pavlova was out of step with her age in her lifetime. By the 1860s the first age of poetry was over. It remained for the later poets Gippius, Akhmatova, and Tsvetaeva to grace—far more illustriously—Russia's next age of poetry.

Notes

[1]In Dorpat, Pavlova became involved with Boris Utin, a law student twenty-five years her junior, who proved to be her greatest love. (Heldt, vi).

[2]Gromov 7.

[3]Pushkin on Pavlov's stories: "Pavlov is the first of us who wrote truly engaging stories." (Gromov, 8)

Pavlov was also among the many leading members of the intelligentsia, including Turgenev, I. and K. Aksakov, Annensky, to sign a letter against the antisemitic slander of two publishers, their protest appeared in *The Russian Herald* (*Russki Vestnik*) in 1858.

V. Lvov-Rogachevsky, *A History of Russian Jewish Literature*, Arthur Levin trans. and ed., (Ann Arbor: Ardis, 1979), 106.

[4]Aleksei Tolstoy arranged for a pension for her from the Russian government. Pavlova translated his works.

[5]Gromov 10.

[6]Other authors she translated include: Scottish ballads, Byron, Thomas Moore, Walter Scott, Goethe, Heine, Schiller, Molière, André Chenier, Hugo, Aeschulus (A scene from Prometheus); Mickiewicz. Franz Liszt set her romance, "Les pleurs des femmes,"(1844) to music and dedicated it to her.

[7]"A Conversation in the Kremlin" sounds the nationalist alarm. It was written in response to her husband's criticism for raising their son abroad, at a time when everyone expected a war with Britain in the Baltic Sea. Pavlova remarked: "I wrote this poem with a Russian feeling in the totally alien city of Derpat." Her adversary Panaev criticized its innovative form, "affected and exotic rhymes," but did not comment on its content. It was also the source of a parody by Rostopchina. (Gaidankov, 566). In 1862, Pavlova wrote "On the Liberation of the Serfs," drawing an analogy to ancient Rome; it concludes with the serf: "Persecuted/he bears the fatal/Mysterious blessing./He brings sacred understanding—/Freedom for future times."

[8]In "Réponse/improvisée en discutant (inutilement) avec une jeune progressiste, Olga Kiréef," Pavlova contrasts the alleged barbarism of ancient times of feudal rule, tallage, and corvée, where the mob was punished by the master with a whip, with the bloodshed of her age, when even shepherds rise up against inequity and oppression. As the play on words of the title suggests, the poem is ironic, with a disdain for materialist or Marxist philosophy: "Je vois l'esprit de dieu traverser les campagnes,/Des pâtres, repoussant l'inique oppression,/Boucher avec leurs corps l'accès de leurs montagnes,/ Des tisserands vainqueurs du maître des Espagnes,/Partout ardent vouloir et puissante action./Et maintenant je vois des faiseurs de systèmes!" (1859)

[9]Martha Dickinson Bianci, quoted by Cynthia Griffin Wolff, *Emily Dickinson*. (New York: Alfred A. Knopf, 1986) 169.

"Sphinx of Oedipus, alas!"

Sphinx of Oedipus, alas! Even now does he
Await the pilgrim on life's path,
Looks him in the eye inexorably
And permits no one to pass.

As of old, even for us, latter-day descendants,
He appears now, fateful
Sphinx of human existence, with one terrifying question,
Half beautiful woman and half beast.

And who among us, believing in himself in vain,
Did not solve the fateful riddle;
He whose spirit has fallen, the claws of the beast await him
In place of the lips of the young goddess.

And the path around is bathed with human blood,
The entire country strewn with bones. . . .
And once again, with a mysterious love,
Already other tribes approach the Sphinx.

1831

For E. M[ilkeev]*

Yes, return to your poor haven:
To the voice of the singer an answer will be given
By the granite of the cliffs and the desolate vale,
Here hearts will not echo in response.

Forget what we had told you,
Abandon what you met for the first time;
Even we could not comprehend you,
And you, a newcomer, did not understand us.

In the silent steppes, at the edge of the world,
Far from human conversations,
There God had cast the poet;
There is no place for him among us.

There no hum of boring conversations,
There the mad foray of a storm,
And the voice of grey and resounding woods,
And the noise of your Siberian rivers.

There under native heavens,
Not knowing our vanities,
Having forgotten us, forgotten by us,
You shall remain a poet!

1838

* Evgenii L. Mil'kiev, (1815–1846/7): a self-taught poet from Western
Siberia who lived in Moscow in the 1840s.

A Sonnet

Do not let the mirror-pure soul grow dim
From their breath, my innocent angel!
As in childhood, reflect with its silver game
All magic tales, gift of the holy days of old.

Marvel at the ruses of the keening mermaid;
May a tousled household spirit appear before you;
Protect the fragrant crown of those enchanting flowers;
Those superstitions are the warrant of love.

Kind maiden, have faith in ancient legends;
In heartfelt simplicity, heed lengthy tales;
Although wise people listen to them and jest,

Be frightened of them in the evening time;
Your soul wanted to be a sister to mine;
For the carefree poet is always a child at heart.

1839

"Yes, there were many of us young girl friends"

Yes, there were many of us young girl friends;
We would often gather together at a childhood holiday,
And the hall would thunder for a long time with our pleasure,
And our circle parted with ringing laughter.

And we did not believe in sorrow or defeat;
We went to encounter life like a bright-eyed crowd;
Splendid and wide, the world shone before us,
And everything that it contained belonged to us.

Yes, there were many of us, yet where's that bright throng?
Oh, each of us discovered life's burden,
And we call that time a fable,
Remembering ourselves as we would a stranger.

1839

A Meditation

The wind blows sorrowfully.
The horizon turns black,
And the moon cannot
Peer out from behind storm-clouds:
And I am sitting alone,
Midst a thick mist,
And not subsiding,
The din of rain rustles like a spring.

And in my soul mournfully
Strength has grown mute,
Sorrow has constrained the heart,
And it seems to me
That everything is in vain,
What we ask for in passion
Is what, appearing clearly,
Lures us in a dream.

It is as if amid the disquiet
Of stormy generations
And pure aspirations
Fruit does not ripen;
It is as if everything holy
In a young heart,
As to the depth of the sea,
Shall fall in vain!

1840

Moscow

Day of quiet reveries, grey and mournful day,
In the sky a rainy mist of clouds,
And in the air the chimes pealing-forth afar,
All the bells of Moscow ringing.

And, summoned by an all-powerful dream,
I remembered suddenly at this time
Another hour, when the evening was clear,
And I was borne along the fields on a steed.

Faster! Faster! and by the edge of a precipice
Having stopped the obedient horse,
I glanced into the expanse of the valleys: glowing,
Already touched by the light of day.

And there the city palatial and cathedral,
Extended far into the distance,
Shining below, as if not made by hand,
And something suddenly was awakened in me.

Moscow! Moscow! What is in this sound?
What heartfelt testimonial does it contain?
Why is it so dear to the poet?
So powerful over the peasant?

Why does it happen that before us
Within you all of Rus awaits us with love?
Why with my eyes shining,
Moscow, do I look at you?

Your palaces stand doleful,
Your sparkle has died out, your voice subdued,
And there is no worldly strength in you,
No thunderous deeds, no earthly blessings.

What kind of secret understandings
Have so taken root in the Russian heart;
Why do your embraces reach,
When you grow pale in the distance?

Moscow! in days of terror and sorrow
Guarding the sacred love,
Not in vain did we give for you
Our life, our blood.

Not in vain in the gigantic struggle
Did the people come to lay down their lives
And fall in the valley of Borodino,
Having said: "Lord have mercy on Moscow."

Blessed was this seed,
It bears its own magnificent flower,
And the young generation shall preserve
The gift of the fathers, the testament of love.

1844

Meditations

Once again, I am here, under the shelter's canopy,
Where I have known so many quiet reveries;
And once again I listen to the whisper
Of familiar cedars and birch trees;
And, as in a bygone spring,
Above their swaying heads,
Cloud after cloud
Floats by from afar.

And once again you float by,
Oh shadows of my best dreams!
Again on the lips irresistibly
A playful poem falls;
Again the subsided anxieties'
Live stream beats in the breast,
And many thoughts and inspirations,
And many songs ahead!

Will I accomplish them? Will I set out bravely,
Where God has deemed me to go?
Alas! The surroundings are deserted,
And replies have fallen silent on the way.
Not during the caprice of poems
Did the poets' round-dance vanish,
And a Russian wind out of nowhere
Does not bring enchanting sounds.

The time came to silence cherished visions;
Because the one who is poor in spirit
Can now disturb with unavailing words
The speechless peace of holy cemeteries! . . .

June 1847

"It was a sparkling sea"

It was a sparkling sea;
Currents of deep blue were singing,
In the open space singing in harmony,
As if they knew my thoughts:
Their consonant melody resembled
Consoling tidings from afar,
Running in from the east, repeating
Their bright swarm one and the same:

And the ninth wave was rolling in wide,
And muttered: "All that's a lie!"

There, in the distance, the morning star rising,
The surge streamed golden in a line;
Through the depth a white-winged bird soared
Toward that band;
And I repeated, with the song of the current,
That I will forget, whirled away there,
About all the sorrow of struggle without purpose,
About all the afflictions of life's chalice.

And the ninth wave was rolling in wide,
And murmured: "All that's a whim!"

Impromptu at the Time of a Versification Lesson

Why are you stumped, Olga Aleksevna?
Why do you gaze, pencil in hand,
At the white sheet so gloomily and in tears?
Tell me, carissima, perché?
Not only every day, but every hour
It's easier for us to thread verses, line to line,
To put together a song, a ballad or eclogue:
Now we are all poets, praise be to God!

And all children are wise and literate
And it's harder for ladies to get on without ink and pen
Than for their great-grandmothers without cosmetic.
A century of greatness and acumen!
Too bad there's no third rhyme in Russian for "etic,"
But what does the poet's ardor leave us?
Some lies—a proud and praiseworthy sign
Of a nature, immensely ingenious.

1859

"I love you, young maidens"

I love you, young maidens;
I love the sorrow of life's spring,
Unclear refrains of a vision,
I love the mysterious dreams
Of the as yet unknowing Eve.

I remember them. In an idle soul
We always remember cherished delirium,
We always remember our false delight,
Both the heart's proud design,
And the sorrow of inner conquest.

For all of us in the midst of life's bondage
Had one and the same dream,
But we, having discovered earthly fates,
We, in whom the passion for pain fell silent
And the heart's whim grew quiet;

We, in whom now there is little strength,
To bear the present,—
We remove the cover
From everything that disturbed the heart,
And shall whisper a quiet: forgive!

1855

Untitled (for Rostopchina)

We are contemporaries, Countess,
Both of us daughters of Moscow,
Bondmaids to vanities; even you
Have not forgotten those days of our youth!

Byron's glory gave life to us,
And Pushkin's oral line of verse.
Yes, it's true, we are the same age,
But not of the same vocation.

You are in Petersburg, in the noisy dale
You live on without obstacles;
You move as you wish
From place to place, from city to city.

Beautiful woman and George-Sandiste,
You sing not for the Moscow river,
And for you, a free artiste,
No one has crossed out a line.

My existence is different; I live at home,
In a crowded and native bound;
Both foreign lands are unknown to me,
As Petersburg is unknown.

In all capitals of various nations
I have not strolled until now;
I do not demand emancipation
And self-determined life;

I love the community and frost of Moscow;
In quiet I accomplish modest work,
And hand over simply to my husband,
My poems for a harsh verdict.

1847
Moscow

Evdokia Petrovna Rostopchina
(1811–1858)

The Poetess Chained to the Ball

"I am a woman! . . . Within me both thought and
    inspiration
Must be constrained by humble modesty."

Rostopchina, "Pushkin's Notebook"[1]

Evdokia Petrovna Rostopchina, née Sushkova, was born in Moscow just months before Napoleon's troops entered the city. Her family escaped to a Simbirsk village, while her father remained in Moscow and was active in the war. Her mother died of consumption when the poet was six; with the financial support of her father, the young girl and her two brothers were raised by their Pashkov grandparents in Moscow.

The Pashkov household seems to have been rather eccentric; the grandfather left his room only to take tea, and the children grew up under a policy of benign neglect that left them relatively independent and free to explore the city. The future poet received a superlative education at home and was well-read in Russian and foreign literature, including Schiller, Goethe, and Byron. She wrote her first poem when she was twelve. When the poet Prince Vyazemsky visited the family in 1830, he arranged for Delvig to publish her "Talisman" in his almanac *Northern Flowers* (1831) to the dismay and surprise of the young girl's family, who considered it somewhat scandalous.

The young Sushkova led the life of a debutante, similar to the one portrayed in Pavlova's *A Double Life*. At the urging of her relatives, in 1833 she married Count Andrei Feodorovich Rostopchin, the reactionary son of the former governor of Moscow who had become a legendary figure for allegedly giving the command to burn Moscow and saved the city from Napoleon in 1812. Whereas marriage was Pavlova's financial nemesis and bane, it brought this poetess into the highest circles of the Russian court and of European society, affording her travels to France, Germany, Austria, and to Italy, whose culture informs her poetry, and which she called the "fatherland of genius." ("Italy.") [2]

41

Rostopchina merits an important place in Russian literary history by virtue of her association with the luminaries of the age. Like any prominent nineteenth-century poetess, like Volkonskaya and Pavlova, the lady of leisure was hostess to male genius. Pushkin, Zhukovsky, Pletnev, Vyazemsky, Sologub, and later the composers Glinka and Liszt, frequented her salon. Gogol visited her in Rome. Lermontov wrote that they were "born under the same star, took the same road, were deceived by the same visions." Even Alexander Dumas requested her memoirs of Lermontov, which were written in French. Herzen quoted her poems in his correspondence. She dedicated many of her poems to contemporary writers; for instance, she wrote "On the Road" to Lermontov, and "A Farewell Song of the Russian Swan" upon Zhukovsky's death, set to his meter and dedicated to his family.

Rostopchina was well-known in the 1830s, frequently publishing in journals and almanacs. Her first collection of poetry appeared in 1841 and received considerable critical acclaim, except from Belinsky, who spoke of her as "chained to the ball." He found her poetry limited in theme, characterized by "introspections and good manners," though he also thought she was "not a total stranger to poetic inspiration." As Barbara Heldt points out, Rostopchina is Pavlova's only significant female rival; the two are "as different" as their respective cities, Petersburg and Moscow, and they occasionally clashed.[3] In "For Countess R.," Pavlova accuses Rostopchina of betraying her native Moscow by describing the ancient city as dead and empty. Rostopchina wrote "A Song about the correspondence of a learned husband and his no less learned wife," based on a polemic between Panaev, Nekrasov's progressive colleague at *The Contemporary*, and Pavlova after "A Conversation in the Kremlin" appeared. This poem is dedicated to Pavlova's son and defends his education in German rather than Russian, against her husband's criticism. Rostopchina, joining in the ensuing debate, borrowed a line from Nekrasov's parody "An avenue of dense-leaved lindens" (the poem is included in this collection).

The countess did not die impoverished or unrecognized like Pavlova, but she did spend the last two years of her life in ill health, subjected to scathing attacks by the utilitarian critics, who called her a "retrograde of the salon," and a "recreant."[4] Rostopchina responded to these attacks in "For my Critics," and in "Vengeance," writing that "a woman is without weaponry," an "unnecessary idol," who when cast down from the pedestal, "avenges herself by consigning those who criticize to oblivion,/but remains pure and faithful to herself." She was condemned by the socialist camp in 1885, twenty-eight years after her death; E.S. Nekrasova called her "immoral, egotistical, demonic and evil" for her aristocratic poetry (*Vestnik Evropy*, March 1885). A conservative and prolific writer of civic poetry, Rostopchina displays both the socialite's outrage and a sense of *noblesse oblige*. In "For Russian Women," she indicts the "vain-glorious women" of her station, and her era, an "iron age," plagued by "the vampire of luxury." Here, the superficial concerns of the beau monde are contrasted with the poverty of the peasant women; she urges the young ladies dressed in satin for the dance in remember the poor women and children in huts; the upper class women's vanity and consumerism have led to chests and shelves crammed with trinkets, bonbonnieres not only the bane of the maid's dusting, but the up-keep of such a life of luxury has led to mortgaging of estates. The upper class is blamed for its lack of concern (after all the peasant's best interest is the grandee's), with a contempt for the up-and-coming merchant class. It concludes with a plea to ladies, too beautiful and kind, to cast off from their haughty shoulders "the madly dear attire,/to feed and clothe the poor." In "Three Queens" she addresses Queen Victoria in the familiar form and blames the British empress, who presides over "incendiary Albion," for revolution and bloodshed throughout Europe.

Ironically, this versifying socialite may have the honor of being among the first Russian women to have a work censored for political reasons. "A Marriage by Force" [not included in this collection] is not just a neo-feminist piece on the constraints of the conjugal institution, as the title suggests, but an allegory of the Russian government's policy toward Poland. Rostopchina composed the ballad when she was in Rome in 1845 and sent it to Russia for publication; Gogol was visiting her at the time and told her no one would guess its true meaning. The piece passed the relatively lax scrutiny of the Tsar's censor and appeared in Bulgarin's journal, *The Northern Bee*. When the allegory was revealed in a foreign paper, Bulgarin's co-publisher was summoned to the Third Section, the government's department for monitoring civic activities and enforcing the policies of the strict reign of Nicholas I. Issues of the journal were recalled and confiscated. The Tsar was outraged and Rostopchina was forcibly removed from a ball. She was not received by the court afterward, and she spent most of her time in Moscow and at Boronovo, her nearby estate.

Although she wrote prose and plays, the most accurate assessment of Rostopchina may be that she was a talented lyricist who mistook her gift for poetry. She composed over forty lyrics, ballads, and songs set to Schubert, Beethoven, and Chopin, as well as to Ukrainian and Spanish melodies. These were sung by Turgenev's inamorata, Pauline Viardot. Her poetry appeared in song-books and was set to the music of contemporary composers, Glinka, Liszt, Dargomyzhsky, and Rubenstein, in whose album her poem "André Chenier" was written. Later, Tschaikovsky used her "Words to Music" ("It's Painful and Delightful") for a romance.

The same woman who chose the pseudonym Clear-Sighted (Woman) for a book, however, never escaped Belinsky's opprobrium. Viewed with condescending feminist hindsight, Rostopchina's poetry needs no parody; her views of women may be curiously original, or clichés of the time. It may indeed make the contemporary reader shudder, though not with the tremors of inspiration so pervasive in her work: "In order to find fascination amid society,/You need to be a woman, or a carefree youth,/To follow without dispute heartfelt attraction/Not to philosophize in vain, to love joyous laughter./Yet I, I am a woman in all meanings of the word,/I am humbly filled with all feminine inclinations;/ I am only a woman,—ready to take pride in this, I love a ball!" Or: "A woman is a restless creation/ Born to dream, to empathize, to love, /To gaze at the heavens/ so that light and trust/will awaken in her timid soul."

Notes

[1]Rostopchina's poems about Pushkin, though notably mediocre and sentimental, provide an interesting portrait of the poet and of the position of a young woman writer. When Pushkin died, Zhukovsky gave her one of his draft books, with a few poems in it, to use for her own writing. In "Pushkin's Notebook," the young woman displays a decidedly female diffidence about her vocation, and her own unworthiness when faced with the pages of genius. While this piece pertains to the history of women writers and their attempts to enter the male domain of poetry, the fate of the notebook may be more interesting than Rostopchina's poem. She later gave it to Lermontov upon his final and fatal journey east to the Caucasus in 1841.

In "Two Meetings," Rostopchina describes seeing Pushkin from a crowd as a child, and her dance with him at Prince Golitsyn's when she met him for the first time in 1828. Having heard the rumor that she wrote, Pushkin "wanted to find out the secret of my thoughts," cheered her "with friendship without flattery." The young socialite takes Pushkin's animated interest as a sincere display of curiosity about a young girl who wants to write and who "had grasped the charms of poetry;" he wanted to hear from her lips "the song of a woman's heart, the song of a woman's suffering," During the dance, while she "whispered poems to him without artfulness, " the great poet listens, inspired, to her "confession."

[2]According to Rostopchina's brother, the marriage was unhappy, primarily because her husband was three years her junior.

44

[3]Heldt, Introduction.

[4]Though condemned by democratic critics, Rostopchina took up the civic call in "A Vision," and "To Those who Suffer," (1827) which she gave a copy of to Sergei Volkonsky when he returned from exile in 1856, and for whom she had given a send-off.

Despite her early tribute to the Decembrists, Rostopchina's later works are more conservative, as in poems upon the death of Nicholas, "To the Russian People," "To the Russian Armory," to the head of the army, Aleksei Ermolov, to the Empress Alexandra Feodorovna, at her request, "A Song to Russian Soldiers Wounded in Sevastopol," arranged for a performance for supporters of their cause at the anniversary of victory over France, and dedicated to the soldiers in the taking of Paris during the Napoleonic wars.

(About Karolina Pavlova)

An avenue of full-leaved lindens,
You are full of meaning for the world!
Aflame with the fire of inspiration
You stood there before him.

And, having bowed your head in pride,
Mightily waving your hand,
You entertained the Lord of Nevsky
With "Masquerade" and "A Double Life,"

And read from a long lowly poem
Your own translation from the Sanskrit . . .
(In Chinese, if not Japanese
This lady publishes poetry!)

Dazed, he gazed at her,
And did not believe his own ears;
And hissed curses through his teeth
To all Queens, all Bluestockings.

Time passed; malice replaced friendship,
A black cat crossed in front of friends.
Treacherous, he forgot what was
In that avenue, where he had feasted!

Of the Queen he published
Malicious criticism in his journal;
And yet she scraped a crushing
Article with her angry pen.

An avenue of dense-leaved lindens,
You are full of meaning for the world!
Inflaming one another with enmity,
Now she and he enrage each other!

For My Critics

I'm not surprised, and really, I'm not angry,
That they rise up against me with such spite:
I would sooner take pride in the journal's maligning,
And slander does not sting my heart.
I have parted with the new generation,
My path diverges from it;
In understanding, spirit and conviction
I belong to another world.
I revere and invoke other gods
And speak in a different tongue;
I am a stranger to them, amusing, this I know,
But I am not embarrassed before their judgment.
I do not seek through crafty incitement
To instigate association with nobility;
I do not want with mystical fondness
And hypocrisy to boast before society;
I do not rush to robbers with embrace,
I do not bring depravity as a gift of praise;
I will not disturb the father's dust with a curse,
And do not write pasquinades of the dead!
Without bitterness, without a murmur, without anger
I look at life, at the world and at people . . .
Because both to the left and right are heard
Anathemas above my head!
A throng of brothers and my friends far away
Has gone to rest, having finished their song.
Unwisely, as a solitary priestess,
I stand before an empty altar!

November, 1856

How Women Must Write

"...de celles
Qui gardent dans leur sein leurs douces étincelles,
Qui cachent en marchant la traces de leurs pas,
Qui soupirent dans l'ombre, et que l'on n'éntend pas."

Joseph Delor

How I love to read others' poems,
To trace in them the growth of the singer's vision
Now to agree with it, then to examine it, to judge,
And denounce it! . . . Vivid fantasies,
And daring thoughts, and the sultry dust of passions;
I question everything with attentive participation,
I put everything to the test; and with all my soul
I share in the singer's rapture, befriend his misfortune,
Love him for his love and trust in it.
But women's poetry attracts me with
Special delight; yet every woman's line of verse
Troubles my heart, and in the sea of my reflections
Affects me with anguish and joy.
Still, I only wish that the modest singer
Would not completely give away her best dreams,
That, modest, she would keep secret and hide
The name of the apparition of her unwilling reveries,
The dear tale of love and sweet tears;
So that only now and then and in gleams
She could allude to feelings too tender . . .
That the stormy shroud of surmises
Always should be above the murmur of hopeless doubts,
Always should she hover mysteriously
Above the song of golden hope; so that the echo of languid
        passion
Would sound trembling under the frame of a modest thought;
So that the heart's fire and sparkle would be covered with cinders,
Like a volcano with lava; so that as an unfathomable depth
Her cherished dream would seem to us;
And that she would be holy for us, as she would be for herself;
Speech not completed with an understanding smile,
Embellished with a warm tear;
The inner impulse forged by the imagination,
Decorum would struggle with enthusiasm,

And wisdom guard every word.
Yes! A woman's soul must shine in the shadow,
Like a lamp's light in a marble urn,
Like the moon at dusk through the cover of storm-clouds;
And warming life, unbeheld, glimmers.

September 22, 1840

Anna Petrovna Bunina
(1774–1829)

Bunina was among the first Russian poetesses to be published and to pursue a literary career with a surprising degree of independence. As a young girl, she won her parents' disapproval by staying in the capital of St. Petersburg on her own, renting an apartment on Vasilievsky island and hiring a servant. Thanks to a small inheritance (600 rubles a year), she studied English, French, German, physics, mathematics and Russian philology under private tutorship. After her funds ran out, she remained in debt and in dire circumstances for the rest of her brief life, suffering from cancer from 1815 until her death in 1829. Her supporters, in particular Admiral Shishkov, implored the Tsar's court on her behalf for a pension, gifts (including a golden lyre made with diamonds), for free medical care; their aid enabled her to seek treatment in Bath, England, where she spent two years (1815–1817).

Bunina's efforts to publish initially met with no success, but in 1806 her first poem, "From the Seashore," appeared in print. Collections of her poetry also were issued: *The Inexperienced Muse* (1809), *Village Evenings* (1811), and a *Complete Works* in three parts in 1819–1821. She also made quite a name for herself by her translations from French, including Batteaux and Boileau, in a collection published in 1821. Toward the end of her life, despite pain that prevented her from lying down, she continued to work, and also translated the Scottish priest and orator Hugh Blair, (1718–1800) whose works were praised by Samuel Johnson and translated throughout all of Europe.

Bunina was strongly influenced by Russian classicism, and in particular by Derzhavin, to whom she dedicated her poem "Evenings." Krylov read her narrative poem "The Fall of Phaeton," at a gathering and apparently she garnered praises from many contemporaries, including Derzhavin and Karamzin, who said: "There is not one woman in our country who has written as strongly as Bunina."

From the Seashore

The bright sea
Flowed from the sky,
In quiet the waves
Lap along the shore,
Brief ripples
Faintly tremble.

The sun's gone down,
There is no moon,
In the scarlet glow
The west is shining,
Birds in their nests,
Flocks in the tree-crests.

Everything suddenly fell silent,
Everything in its place.
In the room it is quiet,
There is no rustle;
The children are nestled
Modestly in the corners.

Lina touched
The strings of the harp;
The golden harp
Gave voice;
Sounds in harmony
Sing with Lina.

In a rose flame
The hearth gives light;
The bright fire
Leaps along the coals;
The smoke dark-silver
Curls in a column.

The fierce flame
scorches the soul;
The heart languishes,
Everything has withered;
Poison flows
In my veins.

Tears ran dry
In troubled eyes,
Sighs stopped
The chest from heaving,
Speech dies down
On cold lips.

Sea, start to churn!
Be a grave for me!
Golden harp,
Strike like thunder!
Fire, flow,
Warm this poor woman!

1806

Nadezhda Sergeevna Teplova
(1814–1848)

Nadezhda Sergeevna Teplova was born in Moscow to a well-to-do merchant family and studied music. At age thirteen she published her first poem, "To the Motherland," an imitation of Zhukovsky's "Golden Harp." Both she and her sister Seraphima, who also wrote poetry, were published in the 1820s in Shalikov's *Ladies' Journal* (*Damskij Zhurnal*). Collections of Teplova's poetry appeared in 1833 and 1838, and posthumously in 1860; the first was reviewed by Belinsky and Kireevsky. From 1837 on she published under her husband's name: Teriuchin. She died in 1848, two years after the death of her daughter and husband. According to Bannikov, Teplova's themes are arch-romantic—often religious and sometimes mystical— and also include "woman's friendship."

The Flute

I love the enchanting radiance of the moon,
And the aroma of lindens, and the light din of branches,
I love the silence of human cares,
I love the speechlessness of passions.
I love the sounds of the sad flute in the evening hour
And I hear their gentle tones
When I bow my head and cross my hands,
The breath held still in my breast.

1835

Autumn

The night wind howls in melancholy,
The pine-forest is hushed, the fields yellowed,
And neither songs nor pipes are heard
In the dark and empty valley.

Crystal currents freeze over,
Their forged sorrow is silent,
And in the sky clouds
Drift by in a stormy row.

Where are you, singers of the heavenly heights?
Already you're no more, your sweet hymn has been sung;
The blossoming groves are deserted,
The last leaves fall from them.

And, the bare trees, swaying,
Give out their mysterious murmur,
And the heart hears their whisper,
The words touch the keen ear.

I do not mourn with gloomy, cold nature,
All, all is now in harmony with me,—
All the while an image of life without joy
And of earthly hopelessness!

October 11, 1835

Julia Valerianovna Zhadovskaya
(1824–1883)

Born in 1824 in the Yaroslavl province, Zhadovskaya lost her mother at a young age and lived with her grandmother in the village of Panfilovo, then in Kostrom with her aunt and in a pension until 1840 when she moved to her father's estate in Yaroslavl. She fell in love with her Russian tutor, P. M. Perevlesky, a philologist of some repute, who also appreciated her poetry. Marriage, however, was forbidden by her father because the man was a deacon's son, for the low clergy were considered beneath the station of the landed gentry. This love became a central theme of her poetry. Visiting Moscow and Petersburg frequently from 1844 on, she met several famous writers; she influenced the poet-democrat L. N. Trefolev. In 1862, she married a physician. Born handicapped, Zhadovskaya became chronically ill at the end of the 1850s, and stopped writing. She died in 1883 at her estate in the village of Tolstikovo in the Kostrom province.

Two of her poems were first published in 1843, and thereafter her poetry appeared in many journals. A collection published in 1846 received some sympathetic reviews in journals, although Belinsky, reviewing her in *Sovremennik,* found her motifs entirely "limited to reverie." A second collection of her poetry in 1858 received more approving reviews by Dobroliubov and Pisarev. She was also the author of novels and stories (*Tales of Julia Zhadovskaya,* 1858). Her last works were *A Woman's Story* and *Woman Abandoned* (1861).

A Storm Cloud Approaching

How fine! In the immeasurable heights
The clouds fly by in rows, turning black . . .
And a fresh wind blows in my face,
Swaying my flowers beside the window;
Thunder sounds in the distance; and a cloud, nearing,
Solemnly and slowly drifts past . . .
How fine! Before a great storm
The anxiety of my soul subsides.

(Between 1844 and 1847)

Field of Grain

Field of grain, my field,
Golden field!
You ripen in the sunlight,
Pouring forth ears of corn.
Wind sends waves coursing
Through your expanse—
As on blue ocean—
Waves ever move.
Above you with songs
A lark cries,
And above you a storm cloud
Passes by, thundering.
You bear fruit and ripen,
Pouring forth ears of corn,
Not knowing anything
Of human cares.
Wind, take away,
The storm cloud,
Protect for us, oh lord,
The working field! . . .

(Between 1856 and 1859)

"A sad picture!"

A sad picture!
In a dense cloud
The smoke hovers from the barn
Beyond the village.
The place is invisible:
Scanty earth,
Flat surroundings,
Fields already squeezed dry.
It is as if all is in mist,
As if everything is asleep . . .
In a thin caftan
A peasant stands,
Nodding his head,
The harvest is bad,
He worries:
How will it be in winter?
Thus all of life passes
With sorrow divided;
And then death comes,
With it the end of labors.
The village priest
Gives communion to the sick man;
They will bring pine cones
From the neighbor's graves;
They will sing the burial rites mournfully . . .
And the old woman, a mother,
For a long time at the grave
Will lament.

(1857)

Poliksena Sergeevna Solovieva (Allegro) (1867–1924)

Solovieva was born in Moscow, the daughter of a well-known historian and rector of Moscow University. Her older brother, Vladimir Soloviev (1853–1900) became a famous philosopher and poet, influential in the future development of Russian literature, particularly Symbolism. Another brother Vsevolod Soloviev was an historical novelist. The household was both intellectual and marked by a devotion to Russian Orthodoxy for both her mother and nanny were devout and her paternal grandfather had been a priest.

Solovieva's biography exemplifies the next generation of women writers after Pavlova who were affected by recent changes in women's education. Unlike the earlier protagonists of Pavlova's *A Double Life* who were taught at home, Allegro not only had the advantages of her father's library and the scholarly atmosphere of the household but also studied painting, sculpture and architecture in school, and voice with famous tutors.

Solovieva published early in *Russkoe Bogatsvo* when she was seventeen or eighteen, and then in *The Herald of Europe* and other journals. Her early poems were read by Fet, a frequent guest of her family. In Petersburg, she knew many prominent writers such as Blok and Ivanov, and frequented many of the famous literary soirées (Sluchevsky's "Friday evenings," as well as Gippius and Merezhkovsky's). She was also a figure in the Crimean literary community and later knew Tsvetaeva and Parnok. With her lover and lifelong companion, the writer N. I. Manaseina, she started a children's journal and publishing house, *Tropinka*. She also translated *Alice in Wonderland*.

Allegro's poetry is not innovative in form. It was primarily written with a male persona and is arch-romantic in its melancholy, solitude, and neoplatonic impulse. "There is no happiness, there is only a reflection of the Unearthly (heavenly) in earthly darkness." Like many of her contemporaries, Allegro viewed the revolutionary events starting in 1905 as apocalyptical, at once a living and threatening force. Reviewing a collection of Allegro's poetry of 1905 (*Rime*), Blok noted that its essential aspects were sorrow and melancholy, and called it "tranquil."Other collections, often illustrated by Allegro, are: *Stikhotvoreniia* (1899), *Plakun-Trava* (1909), *Vecher* (1914), and *Poslednüe Stikhi* (1923).

"Such profound calm"

Such profound calm, serene
In mysterious shadow, amid the grey trunks,
There, in the very depth, where a gentle fern
Has spread the lace of its capricious leaves.

In the sunlight moss glistens gold
And in bright greenery on the grey stump,
In a monotonous, sorrowful note
The cuckoo's cry sounds in profound quiet.

At times a momentary wind drifts past
And is heard in the branches like the sound of the sea;
It is as if the ancient woods respond, awakened
Both from deep dreams and from cherished thoughts.

How fine, having forgotten its sufferings,
To heed the voices of nature amid the quietude
And avidly drink with the soul the ardent kisses
And rays of sunlight, and tender spring!

"In snow—clouds were flying"

In snow—clouds were flying
Pale-faced storms
Out of midnight countries,
And rose up, and swayed,
And with a moan was scattered
The snowy hurricane.
But the snowstorm sang with pleasure,
Tidings of spring to the north from the south
Flow all the while more daring,
Days bright and ungraspable,
And were heeded
Distinct to the loving soul
The cries of cranes.

The Rain

A grey sky and black fir-trees,
The din and breath of rain ...
The heavens could not contain the tears,
Bringing a twilight day.
Moist leaves tired of quivering,
In the weight of their drops of rain.
Evening pensive and filled with sorrow,
Leaving for dark night.
The power of midnight quiet yields,
Just as warriors without a leader
Creep timidly, treading on the roof,
Drops of midnight rain.

1903

Maria Mikhailovna Shkapskaya (1891–1952)

Growing up in St. Petersburg in an intellectual family, Shkapskaya was expelled from high school because of her association with student social revolutionaries and participation in revolutionary activities. Since she was forbidden to study in Russia, she attended an emigré lycée in Paris, where she heard lectures by Henri Bergson and graduated from Toulouse University in 1914.

Despite the political activities of her girlhood, Shkapskaya's poetry is devoid of the revolutionary note of many of her contemporaries, such as Vera Figner. Some of her early lyrics are influenced by Arthurian legends (Lancelot, Tristan) and often exhibit a sense of humor: for example, "A Ballad," a poem about a knight that ends with: "Moral: don't strive for Madonna, and don't enter a convent."

A woman's fate was Shkapskaya's dominant subject, in poems that often resonate with a woman's grief, particularly at the loss of a child. As Boris Filippov points out, she was among the first to handle specifically woman's themes in an innovative manner. Her "thematics are essentially limited to the experience of wife-lover-mother: love, conception, pregnancy, birth or abortion, the death of a child, jealousy, 'a woman's Golgotha,'" as in "Blood Ore" and "Mater Dolorosa." In this respect, "like Vasily Rozanov, she restored in her lyrics the sacred rights of the *flesh.*"[1] This theme recurs even in civic poetry. In *Russia,* her homeland is "a woman, her sister" "autumnal earth lies/Like a woman in labor on the ninth day." She awaits Peter the Great's return, like a lover. Israel awaits Rachel's return ("For Israel"). In "To Louis XVII" (*A Stern Lord's Drum*, title taken from E. Guro), the poet dared in 1921 to express her outrage at the execution of the Tsarevich Aleksei.

Shkapskaya is a poet of great originality. She won the praises of such differing readers as Father Pavel Florensky, who considered her formal mastery superior to Tsvetaeva's and Akhmatova's, and Maxim Gorky, who wrote to her in 1923: "You . . . have taken to a new and very wide road. No woman before you has spoken so truthfully and in so firm a voice of her significance as a woman."(trans. Filippov).[2] She was also a prime example for Trotsky's indictment of the woman writer's religiosity. Her poetry was not published after 1925; as Filippov comments, Shkapskaya's fate was equally tragic—her poetry stopped at the height of her creative powers. She wrote essays and books, devoting her talents to a study of Leningrad factories, and then, as a journalist for *Vechernaya Krasnaya Gazeta,* to the success of workers, including weavers in Samarkand and cotton growers in Tadzhikistan, as well as to Russia's suffering under the Nazi atrocities of World War II.

Notes

[1]Boris Filippov, "Shkapskaya," *Handbook of Russian Literature*, ed. Victor Terras. (New Haven: Yale UP, 1983) 407.

[2]Filippov, 407

The Taiga

In some book—I don't remember,
I read of the white taiga
And since that night I couldn't come to my senses
And my heart was entirely in snow.
And I dream of lands trimmed in fur,
Of soundlessly still waters.
How the quiet flows transfixed
Along their river-bends!
Stubbornly the shaggy
Snow-feathered hills reared,
And the ancient mossy pine-trees
Read the winter psalms.
And all the while more sharp, inexpressible,
The mute distance all the more white,
And from the sky still more incontrovertible
The snowy sorrow falls.

To Louis XVII

1.

I remember with bitter sorrow
How the rats, the bane of childhood days,
Ate up the prison supper
In your small clay cup.

And your lace shirt-cuffs
Tattered at the elbows,
And broken against the door, the nails
Of your pitiful child's hands,

And the faces of the sentry on patrol
And the Temple's narrow, dark courtyard,
And even at the present time I hear
Your bitter, intermittent weeping.

But a mother didn't hold out her gentle hands
To your frightened embraces,
And she is not the one who was roused
By your faint knock on the hollow casemate.

2.

It's nothing new for the people's wrath
To submit to a frightening game.
You, the Seventeenth Louis,
Became a brother to Aleksei the Second.

And he brought his ancient ransom
For the fumes of grievous fires,
Because millions of children were dying
In the villages every year.

For their fathers' tavern revelry,
For the highway covered in blood,

For the crunch of bones in brothers' graves
In Manchurian and other fields.

For the mothers' withered spines,
For the early bitter shine of grey hair,
For Gesya Gelfman,* at the hour of birth-celebration
Of a son taken away by force.

For all of one's brothers disgraced,
For all the graves without markers,
That Rus in the list of prayers for the dead
Has recorded for three hundred years.

For the hot south, for the defeated north,
The law of inexorable bibles,
Executed upon you and him,
Rigorously fulfilled.

But I remember with sorrow and clarity—
I am a mother, and our law is simple:
We did not partake of this blood,
As we did not take part in that other.

1921

*Gesya Gelfman (1855–1882), a woman revolutionary of the 1870s in Kiev,
  member of the People's Will, who died in prison.

Mirra Alexandrovna Lòkhvitskaya
(1869–1905)

Born in Petersburg, Lòkhvitskaya was the daughter of a professor of law; educated at home and then at the Moscow Alexandrovsky Institute, she married an architect in 1892, lived in Tikhin and Yaroslavl, and then in Moscow and was the mother of several children. She died of tuberculosis in 1905, and is buried in the Alexander Nevsky cemetery in St. Petersburg.

Known as the Russian Sappho among literary circles, Lòkhvitskaya represents not only the renewed interest in poetry of the new generation of the 1880s (Apukhin, Nadson, Minsky, Fofanov),[1] but perhaps also the new status of the woman writer. Lòkhvitskaya was a prominent poet, more so than Gippius during her lifetime. She won the Pushkin award from the Academy of Sciences for a collection of poetry in 1896, and a posthumous award was given to her in 1906; she published early, even before finishing school, in 1888, and in 1889, in *Sever*. In 1892 "By the sea" appeared in *Russkoe Bogatstvo*. Her younger sister, Nadezhda, pseudonym Téffi (1872–1952) was also a famous writer, author of poetry and prose, who first made a name for herself in the *Satirikon* journal; like Gippius, she also resigned from the first Bolshevik journal. Teffi moved to Paris in 1920, and became known for ironic and satirical prose works about the life of the emigré.[2]

Lòkhvitskaya's poetry is known for its euphonia, sensuality, and passion, in moods that range from the melancholic, to the joyous and ecstatic, with a symbolist sense of otherworldliness. She later wrote dramatic works, using biblical and medieval themes; her contemporary, Vengerov, wrote that she was drawn to the medieval, fantastic, the "world of witches, and the cult of Satan."[3] As Bannikov noted, her poetry was transitional—she rejected the classical poetics of the nineteenth century, but did not fully work out a new and original style. She was closely connected to Balmont, and also studied with Apollon Maikov—her poetry marks the end of the age of decadence at the *fin de siècle*. Igor Severyanin named her first among his predecessors and tutors, along with Fofanov.

Lòkhvitskaya's poetry offers a great deal for feminist analysis, from her love lyrics that draw from Sappho to her views of woman; in "Learn to Suffer," she urges women to be silent, even when enslaved, and "bearing the mask of the elect."[4] Like Pavlova, she displays a self-consciousness about being a woman writer—but unlike her predecessor, does not convey such marked ambivalence. As Temira Pachmuss puts it, "Lòkhvitskaya insisted on the need for women to express their individuality freely, to lay bare the passionate, erotic aspect of their emotions, to explore and portray elements of their nature which outmoded and stereotyped definitions of 'female' and 'femininity' had excluded."[5]

Notes

[1]Victor Terras, *A History of Russian Literature*, (New Haven and London: Yale UP), 1991, 413.

[2]"Téffi," Temira A. Pachmuss in *A Handbook of Russian Literature*, 465.

[3]Bannikov, 182.

[4]Victor Terras, *A History of Russian Literature*, 414.

[5]Temira A. Pachmuss, "Lokhvitskaya," *A Handbook of Russian Literature*, ed. Victor Terras (Yale UP), 263–4

For my Rival

Yes, I know, she's wonderful,
But even with heavenly beauty
Would she try in vain
To eclipse my golden crown.

Many-columned and vast
My radiant temple stands;
There in the fragrance of idols
The incense of praise does not die down.

There I am queen! I rule
The throng of rhymes, my slaves;
My verse, like a whip, hangs above it
Merciless, and stern.

The singing dactyl in a sultry wave
Replaces my fiery iamb;
Out of restless anapests
I send a bright swarm of trochees.

And strophes in a ringing wave
Run, tame and lithe,
Weaving for my chosen one
Fragrant garlands...

So then pass by! Be off!
Heed weak reason:
Where gods have built their altar,
There is no place for earthly shades!

Oh let them call you more wondrous,
But beauty—a flower of the earth—
Shall fade pale and mute
Before the resounding chord!

(1896–1898)

Zinaida Gippius
(1869–1945)

Zinaida Gippius was active in a climate of intellectual speculation that went beyond what we normally think of as the literary. Her earlier milieu, well portrayed in Andrei Biely's *Reminiscences of Alexander Blok,* included the poet-theologian Vladimir Soloviev—who had been a friend of Dostoevsky—as a dominant figure. The philosophical ideas on the horizon help to explain why Boris Pasternak, a deeply purposeful artist and son of an artist, might later go to Marburg to study philosophy. For Gippius questions about the meaning and bearing of sexuality intersected questions in religion and philosophy as they did saliently in the writings of Vasily Rozanov. They did so notably, too, in Blok's idea of the "Beautiful Lady," the "Prekrasnaya Dama," an idea more complex (as well as perhaps more jejune) than the corresponding notion in most Romantic ideologies. Zinaida Gippius brought all these paths into vibrant intersection and the austere density of her best poems owes its resonance to them as much as to any program of literary expression, though she was also highly literary from an early age.

Born in 1869 into a distinguished family, she was publishing in her teens and accepted by the early practitioners of the "Symbolist" mode. By 1889 she had married the novelist-intellectual Dmitri Merezhkovski. From then on, till his death in 1942, the couple used their apartments in St. Petersburg, Warsaw, and Paris, as a base for various literary, religious, and political activities. They collaborated with Diaghilev in *The World of Art.* Under Gippius' inspiration they founded, together with their vacillating friend Filipov, an alternative church based on a fusion of devotion to the Trinity, a mystical numerology, and a semi-sublimated eroticism. For this they produced a liturgy and regularly celebrated rituals not so different, except for their strange and contradictory privacy, from those of the Russian Orthodox Church they abjured. Later in Paris exile Gippius remained in contact, and usually in controversy, with intellectual theologians, notably Berdyaev.

She and Merezhkovski had already spent the years 1906–1908 in Paris. They left Russia a year after the October Revolution and settled for a while in Warsaw, where they actively sponsored an obscurely defined religious anarchism and mounted various intrigues designed to support the White cause and subvert the Bolsheviks. In 1921 they moved to Paris, where they continued a mix of literary, political, and religious activities, sporadically and idiosyncratically engaging in frequent controversies and beginning a short-lived journal, *The*

New Ship. A philosophical society, *The Green Lamp,* started in 1926, met on Sundays at their apartment till the beginning of World War Two. Finally Gippius became quite isolated, living in penury by the time of her death in 1945.

In her plays *The Red Poppy* (1908) and *The Green Ring* (1914), in her diaries, novels, stories, and other prose writings, as also in her poems, Gippius gave free vent to her opinions on religious and political matters; they were the elements she was sometimes able to distil into achieved poetry. Literary and religious-philosophical matters were combined too in the journal *New Road,* founded in 1902. She intended this journal, like her other activities, to help support what she called "the Cause," the general term for her public activities from then up to the Revolution. Her religious-literary concerns also had a political cast, as indicated by her volume after the 1905 Revolution, *Le Tsar et la révolution* (1907).

The poems characteristically fuse these concerns into sequences of abstractions that are brought to bear on an emotional state. At their best they manage a middle ground between the poet's own doctrines and the refined postures of such late romantics as Tiutchev. They dramatize what they precipitate, the poised statement about the impossibility of attaining poise, the lovelorn core of the unachievable desire to love. They rise to austere measurement, as Innokenti Annenski said of them, evidencing "a certain absolute momentariness, a certain present, glowing need to communicate rhythmically the full sensation of the moment, and with that its strength and charm." These are very general attributions, but will serve well to distance Gippius somewhat from such associates as Blok, whose poems offer a more distinct program and greater play but no more well-bounded condensation than Gippius at her best. Or, at another angle, speaking of such immediate predecessors as Gippius but in terms broad enough to include Baudelaire, Mandelshtam offers a properly paradoxical assessment, "But the Decadents were *Christian* artists . . . For them the music of decay was the music of resurrection." In Gippius such music is distinct, if often faint.

Traditional in the rhetorical set and emotional gesture of her poems, as also in their form, Gippius is modernist in the ellipses and intensities of her best work. Her abstractions of image hover on the edge of the absoluteness that is more fully achieved in the clear outlines of Akhmatova, the murky prisms of Blok, and the revelatory disjunctions of Pasternak, to speak only of her Russian contemporaries.

Radiances

Radiance of words. Does such exist?
Radiance of stars, radiance of clouds—
I loved them all, I love them, but if
They tell me, here is the radiance of words,
I answer, without fear of the avowal,
That even sanctity's blest radiance
I am ready to give up for that,
All for the radiance of words alone.

Radiance of words? Should I repeat to you
Once again, my poor fellow poet,
That I am speaking of the radiance of the Word,
That on earth there are no other radiances?

Night Flowers

Oh, do not trust the hour of night.
It is full of evil beauty.
That hour people are close to death
And only strangely are flowers alive.

Dark, warm silent walls
And a hearth long without fire . . .
And I wait for perfidy from flowers—
The flowers are detesting me.

Among them I am hot and anxious.
Their aroma is heady and bold—
But I cannot go away from them,
But I cannot escape their shafts.

The light of evening rays strikes
Across blood-red silk on the leaves.
A tender body comes to life,
There have awakened evil flowers.

From a poison Arum lily measured
Drops are falling on the rug . . .
All mysteriously, all faithlessly,
And a silent strife I seem to hear.

They are rustling, stirring, breathing,
Like enemies they pursue me.
All that I think they know and hear.
And they desire to poison me.

O, do not trust the hour of night!
Shore yourself from the evil beauty.
This hour we are all closer to death,
Only the lone flowers are alive.

The Chain

Alone I go, go across the snowy square
In the lightly misting evening gloom
And think a single thought, a mutinous one,
One always senseless, always full of desire.

The bells are still, cathedral bells are still,
And the chain barrier is less mobile in the gloom,
But past the chain, far, like dark shadows
Like apparitions these neighbors draw near.

They are coming, beautiful and hideous,
They are coming merry, they are coming sad;
They are so alike, so various,
So near at hand, so far away.

Where are the hated ones, where are the dear?
Are the same paths not readied for them all?
Like dark links, inseparable,
We are forged forever in a single chain.

Green, Yellow, and Blue

I am sadly exhausted.
I am weak without reply.
O world of such varied sound,
Of such grossly varied light.

To a question in confidence—
Offensive answers.
All is mixed up—by accident,
Words, flowers, and lights.

I understand the icon-lamp,
The green icon-lamp,
The stains of the yellow lamp
Are a barrier for its rays.

And, blue, the windows
Were congealed with gleaming ice.
Rays interwove in the fibres,
Of murky, brown dust.

And people, evilly, variously
Interflow, like stains,
Senselessly, hideously,
And grossly inscrutable.

Impotence

I look at the sea with greedy eyes,
Rivetted to the earth at the shore . . .
I stand above the abyss—above the skies—
And I cannot fly away to the blue.

I'm not sure whether to rebel or resign.
I have courage neither to live nor die.
God is near me—I cannot pray,
I want love—and I am unable to love.

To the sun, to the sun I stretch out my arms,
And I see a curtain of pallid clouds . . .
It seems to me that I know the truth—
And it's just for that I don't know the words.

Electricity

Two wires are woven together,
Their endings are exposed.
This "yes" and "no" are not fused,
Not fused but spliced.
Their dark splicing
Is tight and deadly.
But resurrection awaits them,
And they await it.
Endings will touch endings—
Other "yesses" and "Noes."
And "yes" and "no" will wake,
Their splicings will merge,
And their death will be—Light.

Leeches

There where the creek is quiet, the current is still,
Black leeches stick to the root of the reed.

In the fearful hour of enlightenment, at the sunset of day,
I see leeches sticking onto my soul too.

But the soul is weary of the deathly silence,
Leeches, black leeches of greedy sin.

She

In her unscrupulous and sorry meanness
She is gray like dust, like the ash of earth.
And I am dying from this nearness
Of her inextricability from me.

She is rough, she is prickly,
She is cold, she is a snake.
Her repulsive, scalding, intercoiling
Scales have wounded me all over.

O, would that I could just feel a sharp sting.
She is flaccid, dull, still.
So lumpish she is, and so inert,
And there is no approach to her—she is deaf.

She in her coils stubbornly
Fawns on me, crushing me.
And this deadly thing, this black thing,
This fearful thing—is my soul!

Zinaida Gippius

Petersburg

I love you, handiwork of Peter.

Your frame is straight, your outline cruel,
Harshly dusty is your grey granite,
And each unstable street crossing
Trembles with dull perfidy.

That cold boiling of yours is more
Fearful than deserts' immobility,
Your breath is death and decay,
Your waters a bitter wormwood.

Like coal your days. Your nights are white.
A corpse-like gloom strains from your public gardens,
And the glassy firmament is transfixed
By a needle from across the river.

It happens: the water's current is turning,
Rearing up, the river goes backward.
The river will never wash off the rusty stains
From the granite mass of its banks.

Those stains of rust are boiled on,
They can't be forgotten or trodden down.
It burns, burns on the dark body,
Their inextinguishable imprint.

As before, your bronze serpent coils.
Over the serpent chills the bronze horse,
And a victorious, all-purifying
Fire will not gobble you up.

No! You will drown in your black muck.
Cursed city, enemy of God,
And the worm of the swamp, the stubborn worm
Will eat up your skeleton of stone.

Measure

Always there is something not there,
And something too much.
To everything there would be an answer,
But without a last syllable.

Something happens—it's not so;
It's out of place, fragile, unstable . . .
And each sign is untrue,
In every solution's a fault.

The moon snakes on the water,
But the road, the golden one, lies . . .
Damage, whiplash everywhere.
But the measure—is only with God.

At Night

At night I know strange revelations
When I go to meet the stillness,
When I love the contacts of its touch
And a clear strength grows in me.

Does my soul conjure or pray,—
I know not, but it's a joy for me to know.
I feel time is broken in half
And the future will be what it is.

All hopes—all distance and nearness
Are confined in one big circle.
Like a fiery wind are my desires,
Like a wind, uncontained and strong.

And I see on someone white haloes
Catch fire with a new radiance.
Over times, in me, there come in contact
The beginnings and the ends.

Glass

In the country where all is unusual
We are tied in a winning mystery.
But in our life, not accidentally,
Disconnecting us, there lay
Between us a dark glass.
I am unable to break the glass,
I do not dare to call for help.
Leaning on the dark glass
I look upon the cheerless gloom
And the glassy cold is fearful to me.
Love, love! O give me a hammer,
Let the shards hurt, no matter what.
We will remember just one thing,
That there where all is unusual
Not by our will, not accidentally,
We are tied in the last mystery.
God will hear. It is daylight all around.
He will give us strength to break the glass.

Non-love

Like a damp wind you beat upon the shutters,
Like a black wind you sing: You are mine!
I am ancient chaos, I am your old friend,
Your only friend. Open up, open up!

I grasp the shutters, I do not dare open.
I clutch the shutters and hide my dread.
I keep, I cherish, I keep, I desire
My final gleam, my love.

The chaos laughs, it calls out, eyeless:
You will die in fetters—break them, break them.
You know your fortune,—You are lonely.
In freedom is fortune—and in Love-lack.

Being chilled, I fashion a prayer.
I just manage to fashion a prayer of love.
My hands are weakening, I end the battle,
My hands are weakening, I'll open up!

September's

There are towels of a moon green
On the white window, on the floor.
But a yellow candle's been prayed with
Under the heather there in the corner.

I rub off the misted window.
With two lights in white I write
Of green, yellow, white!
What shall I choose, what decide?

At the Sergeyevsky

My window is low, upon the street,
Low and open wide,
The ore-sticky pavement so close
Under the window, exposed wide.

On the pavements are street lamp spots,
All over the pavements, people, people . . .
And bustle and howl and screech
And in the rushing, people, people . . .

Like the pavement are their clothes and faces,
They, the living and the dead—are together.
It is years, years flowing by—
That the living and the dead are together.

Against them I will not shut the window.
I myself, am I alive or dead?
All's the same, I howl at them,
All's the same, living or dead.

There's no fault, and no one to answer.
No answer for the nether world.
We thought that we live in the world,
But we fight, fight in the nether world.

Here

Let it be I dreamt it, the strange long evening.
I remember this evening all the same.
The outpouring of dawn is wine-green,
A big semicircular window.
And somewhere in the window, in the near distance
Such a melodious stillness
And a parting at the low door,
A cherished, star-decked country.

Your words in farewell, simple,
The last words, forget, be still,
And they were strewn, icy,
Unbearably sharp rays.

Love's holy irrevocability,
And thou and I, we remembered together
And impossibility became impossible
Here on earth, through falsity and pettiness,
Touching love with a clean spike.

The Past

You fell out of love—why?—to stroll with me
Over a hard and bristly field
Going as a couple no matter where
To look at the rye, high as I am,
To speak of something half accidentally
Lightly and cheerfully, somewhat forbidden,
And suddenly under a rosy chain of mountains,
Under a white moon not kindled yet,
To see the sea, a blue semicircle
Of mysterious waves more dazzling than a flame . . .

To go back, to go forward, thither,
Where the warm rainbow's smoky-hot pillar
Holds up from below the sunset cloud . . .
And on one raincoat to take a rest,
Walk further on and discuss Dante,
Of you and of a married Beatrice.
But to go still amid the leafy temple
In the marvelous gloom of its straight columns
Under the chaste and stern caress
Of the light of street lamps. Strange, the reason
You fell out of love? . . . No, I smile,
I understand.

Mirrors

But you never did see?
In garden or park—I don't know,
Everywhere mirrors shone.
Down there, in the clearing, at the edge,
Above, in the birches, in the firs,
Where leapt the gentle squirrels,
Where bent the shaggy branches.
Everywhere mirrors dazzled.
And above—the grasses swayed,
And below—the clouds ran . . .
But each one was cunning.
Little to them was earth or sky—
They repeated one another,
They reflected one another . . .
And in each one—dawn's rosiness;
Merged from the green grass;
And they were, in the mirror's twinkling,
Earth's or heaven's—the same.

Silence

On the streets a white silence.
I do not hear my heart.
Heart, why are you quiet?
Such a still, such a still silence . . .

The town is snowy, white,—arise.
The moon is a bloodied shield.
The coming time's known less and less.
My heart, arise, arise.

Resurrection is not for all.
The still snow is still as if dead.
Sin spreads out over the town.
Stilly I weep, I weep for all.

Womanhood

Falling, falling lines.
Woman's soul is unconscious.
Is much needed for it?

So be as I shall be from now on,
Quietly attentive to woman,
More caressingly, more tenderly.

Woman's soul—a desert.
Does it know how cold it is?
Does it know how gross?

Placate the innocent soul.
Delude it that it is free.
All the same it will be a slave.

Marina Tsvetaeva
(1892–1941)

"In a word, the *precise* feeling is: there is *no place* for me
in modernity."

Marina Tsvetaeva
January 1, 1932[1]

" . . . To tell the truth, I have been a stranger in *every*
circle, all of my life. It's the same among the political
people and the poets. My circle is the circle of the universe
(of the soul as well) and the circle of the human being, his
human solitude, separation. And also, I forgot! the circle
of the plaza with the tsars (with leaders, heroes)."[2]

A native of Moscow, later a resident of Prague and Paris, Tsvetaeva
lived the myth of journey, exile, and tragic return. In *Requiem,* Anna
Akhmatova asserted her place in the Stalinist Terror as aligned with
her people, not under a "stranger's" firmament. And on her return
to Soviet Russia Tsvetaeva was to find herself standing on the same
lines as the women of Akhmatova's tribute, where the acceptance of
a package indicated that someone was still alive.[3]
    Tsvetaeva's father, the philologist and professor Ivan Tsvetaev,
founded the Alexander III Museum, now renamed the Pushkin Museum, in Moscow. The plaque with his profile on the façade of the
building underscores the fundamental ironic position of his daughter
in the former Soviet Union; until the recent change in cultural climate enunciated as *perestroika,* the great poet had had no such sign-
post or tribute; even the exact location of her grave is unknown.
The poet believed in her own matrilineal *daimon* or genius for famil-
ial devotion and sacrifice.[4] Her sense of duty and her role as a mother
inform her entire life and find deep resonances throughout her poetry, not only in her many poems that celebrate her children.
    Boris Pasternak describes Tsvetaeva:

Of course, she was more Russian than all of us, not only in
her blood . . . but in the rhythms that inhabited her soul, in
her tremendous, uniquely powerful language . . . She lived
an heroic life. She accomplished prodigies every day. They
were prodigies of loyalty to the only land whose citizen she

[ever] was—[the land of] poetry. (translated by Robin Kemball)[5]

During the Civil War, Tsvetaeva's husband, Sergei Efron, went off to fight in the White Army and Tsvetaeva was left with two young daughters. The younger one, Irina, whom she had to place in a children's home to survive, died of malnutrition in 1920, during the two months Tsvetaeva was nursing her elder daughter Ariadna who had malaria. The couple was reunited in Berlin in 1922 and from then on she supported the family, largely on stipends from the Czech government, while he pursued his career as a student, occasionally working in publishing or as an extra in films. While they were living in France in the late twenties and early thirties, Efron became involved with émigré leftist political circles. Their daughter Ariadna decided to go back to the country she had left as a child and did so in 1937. Efron, the former White Army officer, was more than a Soviet sympathizer; he became a Stalinist agent abroad. He was implicated in the assassination of a Soviet defector in 1937 and fled the country via Spain. Years later it turned out that he was also instrumental in the 1936 assassination of Trotsky's son, Lev Sedov. Tsvetaeva, ignorant of his involvement and of his whereabouts, was nevertheless arrested and interrogated by the French police. After hours of questioning, she recited French poetry, both her own, and tragedies, in response. She also remarked, "La bonne foi d'Efron a pu être surprise . . . ma foi en lui reste intacte."[6]

With her daughter and her husband already in the Soviet Union, and her son insisting on returning, Tsveteva herself went back in June of 1939. On the eve of her departure, she re-entered in her notebook the now famous line of 1918 that she had once vowed to follow Efron "like a dog" should he survive the Revolution. The reunion took place at an NKVD (precursor of the KGB) safehouse.

During the first year back, Efron was arrested, as were Tsvetaeva's sister Anastasia and her pregnant daughter Ariadna, who was beaten during the interrogation. She spent the next seventeen years in prison camps. Efron's fate is unclear. He died either during interrogation or in the camps. With the onset of World War II, Tsvetaeva and her son were evacuated to the Tatar town of Elabuga. She committed suicide on August 31, 1941.

Tsvetaeva the woman was outspoken, confident, defiant. Nadezhda Mandelshtam wrote of her "absolute directness and stunning wilfullness."[7] She was the kind of woman who could read a cycle of verse in praise of the White Army to Red Army soldiers and be applauded. She could as easily write a poem to People's Commissar Lunacharsky, who helped her during the Civil War years, that there

is a more important law, that of "the extended hand, the open soul,"
adding: "And we shall be judged—know this,/by one measure./And
there will be for both of us—Paradise,/In which I do believe."("Your
banners are not mine!")

Anti-political and thus anti-Soviet by conviction, Tsvetaeva's poetry speaks to the moral chord of poetry; as she remarked, hunger is
also political. Nor did she let politics stand in the way of appreciat-
ing art. She agreed, for instance, to publish in *Volia Rossii* (*Freedom
of Russia*), the journal of the Socialist Revolutionaries in exile, simply because its office was where Mozart composed *Don Giovanni*.[8]
When Vladimir Mayakovsky, the self-appointed spokesman in poetry of Soviet ideology whom Stalin praised posthumously, gave a
reading in Paris, Tsvetaeva was asked by the émigré press what she
thought. She replied: "The strength is over there." While she was
referring to poetry, the remark was misconstrued as political praise
and she was criticized in the conservative press. As she noted, her
poetry was too radical in form for the conversative press, and too
conservative in content for the progressive publishers.[9]

Tsvetaeva, who lived through her poetry and defined her self
through it, considered it a terrain above the level of *byt* (everyday
existence) and beyond the categories of gender. She may be the most
elliptical and elusive of the Russian poets of her generation,
placelessness the dominant chord of her life. Literally a displaced
person in a life of emigration, Tsvetaeva was an insider only in poetry. As she wrote in a letter of 1925: "I don't like life as such, for
me it begins to have significance, i.e., to take on sense and weight—
only when transfigured, i.e., in art. If I were taken beyond the ocean—
into heaven—and forbidden to write, I would reject both the ocean
and heaven. For me *the thing itself* is not necessary."[10] Her view of
the poet also reflects the influence of German romanticism and Russian symbolism. "Any poet is by nature an emigrant, even in Russia.
An emigrant of the Kingdom of Heaven and of nature's earthly paradise," she wrote in her essay "The Poet and Time."

As the poet in exile, Tsvetaeva follows in the tradition of Russian
poets like Pushkin, but for her the homeland no longer existed:

> If I were in Russia, everything would be different, but there
> is no Russia (the sound) there are the letters: SSSR,—I just
> can't go to a *toneless*, vowelless, [hissing] thicket. I'm not
> joking, just the thought alone is stifling. Besides, they won't
> let me into Russia: *the letters don't move apart*. (Open
> Sesame!). In Russia, I'm a poet without books, here, I'm a
> poet without readers. What I do isn't necessary to anyone."[11]

Tsvetaeva's audacity was significant enough to make her a highly controversial figure in both the Soviet Union and the West. She was misrepresented, misunderstood, and unpublished in the USSR.

Tsvetaeva became an emblematic figure of the writer antithetical to Soviet ideology. The process began early, in the more tolerant twenties. In 1921, Meyerhold declared the obvious and called her hostile to the Revolution. In *Literature and Revolution* (1923), Trotsky criticized Tsvetaeva and Akhmatova among others for the "feminine religiosity" of their poetry.[12] In the 1934 edition of the Great Soviet Encyclopedia, Tsvetaeva was accused of "glorifying the Romanov family, while her manner of writing verse had degenerated into naked rhythmic formalism."[13]

In her exile Tsvetaeva's talent was acknowledged by Pasternak and Rilke, but others who shared her displacement in Soviet Russia failed to appreciate her works at the time. After her death Akhmatova stated that she had not fully recognized her talent. Even Vladimir Nabokov, who once met Tsvetaeva and took a stroll in the mountains with her, said likewise.

In an early lyric, Tsvetaeva confidently put acclaim for her verse in the future perfective. She is now only beginning to receive the attention she deserves. Banned for decades in the USSR, she has been gradually rehabilitated since the 1960s by the publication of collections of her verse, in memoirs, and through scholarly studies about her.

A diversified and prolific craftswoman, Tsvetaeva was not only a poet but a dramatist, an essayist, a critic, and a correspondent of and with genius. As western Slavic scholarship has made Tsvetaeva's works available only recently, we are just beginning to appreciate the full range of her works. She described herself as at least seven poets. Within her poetry alone there is a wide range of styles: early conventional lyrics, romantic and symbolist imagery, folkloric forms, modernist and Cubist displays, and the later complex narrative *poemas*. Literary subtexts and echoes are also common in her poetry. Among the sources and influences she uses are German and Russian folklore and legends (*bylyny*), Classical myths, and Neoclassical drama. In her prose of the 1930s, as J. Marin King points out, Tsvetaeva succeeds in "combining the mythic with the historico-biographical." She manages "to bring the legendary into the workaday world."[14] Also a gifted translator from Spanish, French, German, English, and Georgian, she wrote poetry in French and German.

Tsvetaeva has been accused of hero-worship, nostalgia, and sentimentality. While the irretrievability of time-past and the loss of home and homeland dominated her life, sentimental complaint or self-pity is curiously absent from her works, even in "Homesickness". Her dominant cadence, with its timbre of uplift and descent, is strangely affirmative. The first-person voice often conveys a vitality of self, an urgent musical cadence and restless inquisitiveness, no matter the identity of the persona. Tsvetaeva is many-voiced: breathless, angry, poignant, indignant, delighted, outraged and defiant, or contemptuous. ("Readers of Newspapers."). She is a poet of her era, born of the urban, her voice often a diatribe against urbanity and contemporary events. In *Poems to Czechoslovakia,* for example she writes: "I refuse to be/In an inhuman Bedlam/I refuse—to live/With wolves of the squares/I refuse to howl/With sharks of the ravines/I refuse to swim—Downstream/With the tide of spines. . . .") Tsvetaeva dares to experiment radically in versification. She extends the romantic dialectic by exploring the fluid or discordant associations of a word's sound or image, often in an exclamatory note; for example, the use of harsh sybillants and objects that enforces a sense of a woman's domestic entrapment in a dialectic against that other life in "Life's Train," not included in this anthology. She boldly uses the exclamation point, so often a sign of sentimental cliché, as a point of departure.

One could well focus on Tsvetaeva by considering her "Attempt at a Room." This poem was written in 1926 and published in 1928 in the émigré journal *Volya Rossii,* the same year as Virginia Woolf's famous essay on the same theme. Tsvetaeva was literally writing from a woman's historic place, under the conditions that Woolf gives as reasons by themselves for women's inability to write—and Tsvetaeva had the added burden of supporting a family. Unlike Woolf's fictional Renaissance maiden, however, Tsvetaeva was not squelched by her social or economic conditions, or by the drudgery of daily living (*byt*), for which she had a lifelong contempt. While the English writer was comfortably lamenting the state of the arts for women in Bloomsbury, the Russian poet had to pay for the midwife and for medicines after the birth of her son, and scrounge for second-hand baby furniture. She wore one woolen dress all winter and had to ask a friend for a washable one, "because a snake must change its skin." [15] Her friend, Elena Izvolskaya describes her:

It's possible to write about Tsvetaeva as a poet, as a prosaist. It's possible to write about the woman who perished tragically in a Soviet trap. It's possible to write about her as the wife of Sergei Efron, who confirmed the frightening prediction of Dostoevsky, and became possessed and perished with the devils. But there is also however *simply* Marina, the one who lived among us in Meudon, and never guessed Serezha's dark actions and terrifying temptations (we who knew her then can attest to this; she never guessed, because she lived in her very own world, *far* from all of them, even from those who were closest to her). I can write only about *this* Marina, for really there was no other. This is *my* Marina, the one who worked and wrote, and gathered firewood, and fed her family scraps. She washed, did the laundry, sewed with her once slender fingers, now coarsened by work. I well remember those fingers, yellowed from smoking, they held a teapot, a saucepan, a frying pan, a pot, threaded a needle, and lit the stove. These same fingers guided the pen or pencil across a sheet of paper, on the kitchen table, from which everything had been cleared in a hurry. At this table Marina wrote, poems, prose, she sketched drafts of entire long poems, sometimes she would sketch two, three words, and some kind of particular rhyme, re-writing it *many, many* times. This was the law of her art.[16]

Tsvetaeva's poem relies upon the conceit—now a conventional symbol for women—of the room alone, that is emblematic of a writer's psychological state. As Tsvetaeva wrote in a letter of that summer, "a room is freedom."[17] But her attempt is not simply motivated by the desire for new lodgings, nor is it meant to reflect a feminist social consciousness. Here the poet focusses on an inner eternal life. Throughout the poem she strives to create a fictive construct for a metaphysical meeting-ground with kindred poets. (It is addressed to both Pasternak and Rilke.)[18] As Simon Karlinsky has pointed out, it is surreal and "dream-like," its main theme a "fusion" that combines the spiritual and erotic.[19]

"Attempt at a Room" is based on a paradoxical conceit. Tsvetaeva subverts the confines of three-dimensional time-space through the vehicle of poetry. The tone is highly playful, relying primarily upon tricks of perception, the optical illusion of the mirror that transports the poet. With the collapse signaled in the opening lines, the poet refers to the rupture of cultural revolution (the Tsar's abdication) and moves back through time. Spatial relations are altered: the opening walls of a room collapse and become a piano player's back, a film-like screen displaying Pushkin's duel, the scene of execution; hotel corridors become internalized chambers of a heart.

The poem is written in a fluid stream-of-consciousness narrative in a process of association where sound-play, the resonance of an image or word, often determines the next sequence. In fact, sound was central to her aesthetic, as she wrote when recalling her poem of a White Army soldier that won popularity as being about a Red Army officer: "There is something in poems that is more important than their meaning: their sound."[20]

In its preoccupation with time-space, and its self-conscious play on perception, "Attempt at a Room" epitomizes various aspects of modernism: constructivism, surrealism, suprematism, montage, and other devices of film. Here Tsvetaeva, dispelling any misconceptions about her work as nostalgic in theme, reveals a modernist sensibility. Like the Cubist and Futurist painters, the poet also consciously draws analogies to other media, incorporating them into her work in ways that only language or imagination permit. The fourth wall implied in the opening not only marks the entrance into a fourth-dimensional zone of time as memory and metaphysical space; it suggests the open fourth wall of the stage. The image of the piano player is carried through by the musical sound-play of the rhymes and the poem is compared to a sketch, with its shading suggesting a painting like Malevich's "White on White." At its conclusion, the metaphor of deconstruction is realized with a collapse of language as well. The poet stands precariously triumphant on a hyphen, the space of ellipsis.

In his essay, "Footnote to a Poem,"[21] Joseph Brodsky calls "New Year's Greetings" a "landmark" in terms of both Russian poetry and Tsvetaeva's poetry. Written upon Rilke's death, it is both an elegy and an address. Here Tsvetaeva has relied upon the private context of their correspondence making many allusions to Rilke's poetry including his "Elegy to Marina Tsvetaeva," in which he calls lament a "descending joy." The word "Rai" in Russian (Heaven or paradise) is contained in Rainer Rilke's name and the poet builds on this in the sequence. Here she also alludes to Orthodox liturgy and Greek mythology. As in "Attempt at a Room," Tsvetaeva aims toward a meeting with the poet in that other world, the hereafter. There is an implicit allusion to Eurydice and Orpheus meeting in the hereafter. This is also a theme of "Attempt at a Room,"and one of the poem's threads that derives from Rilke.

Further adding to the enigma of her poetry is Tsvetaeva's use of ellipsis and paranomasia in a poetics also marked by an astonishing clarity. Akhmatova called her "dolphinlike" in reference to her later poetry.[22] Tsvetaeva often utilizes what Roman Jakobson calls the poetry of grammar: enigmatic ellipses and paranomasia that make a slight change in grammatical case or shift in verbal aspect from the previous line to determine the next sequence. Here, as elsewhere, Tsvetaeva proclaims, exclaims, declaims, moving along the musical clef of her verse, taking the word to heights in elegiac lament, and to the very edge, as ellipsis incorporates its silent counterpart. The poet moves toward the silence of death, while digressing away from the poem's substance. The poet's voice is a dialogic defiance, the figure of Rilke located in a stillpoint. An antinomial stance also underscores the central irony of the poem: to write about Rilke is to limit him, to articulate the ineffable is to fail to do so. Thus what is unspoken or unsung is a central part of the poem. Tsvetaeva's characteristic ellipsis underscores the philosophical paradox and confirms her rightful place in modernity.

Notes

[1]Marina Tsvetaeva, *Pis'ma k Anne Teskovoj* (Jerusalem: *Versty*, 1982) Letters No. 76, 97.

[2]Letter to Teskova, January 3, 1928, 59.

[3]Simon Karlinsky *Marina Tsvetaeva: The Woman, her World and her Poetry* (Cambridge: Cambridge University Press, 1985), 230.

On Tsvetaeva's biography, I am following primarily Karlinsky, and his earlier *Marina Cvetaeva: Her Life and Art* (Berkeley: University of California Press, 1966) as well as Carl R. Proffer's introductory essay "Tsvetaeva: A Biographical Note" in J. Marin King, ed. and trans., *A Captive Spirit: Selected Prose* by Marina Tsvetaeva (Ann Arbor: Ardis, 1980).

Many of the facts of Tsvetaeva's and her family's biography remain to be clarified, pending research and access to documents only made recently available in the former Soviet Union. The poet also specified that her archives be closed until 1999.

[4]Letter to Testova, Jan. 26, 1934, No. 65, 109–110.

[5]These remarks from Pasternak's conversation with Alexander Gladkov, February 20, 1942, as recalled by Gladkov, are quoted in translation in "*The Demesne of the Swans*— A Tale within a Tale," introd. Robin Kemball's bilingual edition of Marina Tsvetaeva, *The Demesne of the Swans* (Ann Arbor: Ardis, 1980), 27.

[6]Kemball, 20.

[7]Nadezhda Mandelshtam, *Vtoraiia Kniga*, 517–518.

[8]Karlinsky (1985) 127.

[9]Kemball 16.

[10]Letter to Teskova, No. 20, Dec. 30, 1925, 37.

[11]Letter to Teskova, undated from 1928, No. 40, 61–62.

[12]Simon Karlinsky (1985), 130–131.

[13]Quoted and translated by Karlinsky (1985), 201.

[14]J. Marin King, ed. and trans., "Introduction", Marina Tsvetaeva, *A Captive Spirit: Selected Prose* (Ann Arbor: Ardis, 1980), p. 19.

[15]No. 5 of Feb. 10, 1925. As Karlinsky notes, an English translation of Tsvetaeva's letter to Teskova of December 12, 1927 appears in Michele Murray, ed., *A House of Good Proportion: Images of Women in Litertaure.* (New York: 1973).

[16]Elena Izvolskaya, "Ten, na stenakh," *Opyty*, 1954 III, 155–156.

[17]Tsvetaeva wrote to Teskova:

Now,—in the present situation of 1,000 a month, is it possible for me to hope, dear Anna Antonovna, to live on that kind of money *in Prague?* How I would like to be near you! It must be an absolutely decent region (I'm thinking about the children, for I love factories and train stations as the most sorrowful of places), nearby garden for taking walks. I would like to be in Prague, but not in the suburbs, in order to live more like a human being,— not just as a soul and unskilled worker. But I'm constrained by the children and the money. Have you thought of something concerning a room? A room is freedom, but is it expensive? Inaccessible? Would it not be possible to find two rooms with Czechs who like Russians and aren't too strict about order? The best would be one with a cleaning woman (I would pay for a servant), maybe also including dinner? (Only not at a general table!) In Czechoslovakia, it's possible to live like a human being, I was living not as a human being and am tired of living so, tired too early.

(No. 24, of July 20, 1926.)

[18]After Rilke's death, Tsvetaeva wrote to Pasternak: "The verse about you and me . . . turned out to be verse about him and me, *every line.* A curious substitution occurred; the verse was written in the days of my extreme concentration on him, yet it was directed— consciously and willfully to you. It turned out to be less about you. It turned out—to be less about him!—about him now (after December 29th), i.e., in anticipation, by insight. I was simply talking to him (as if he were) alive, for whom *I didn't intend it,*— since we didn't meet, since we met *otherwise.* Hence also at that very time my strange, distressed . . . state of not loving, estrangement, *rejection* in every line. The piece is called "Attempt at a Room," and I kept resisting it at every line. Read it carefully, read into every line, *check* it." Letter of 2/9/1927, quoted in: *Stikhotvoreniia i poemy v piati tomakh,* (New York: Russica, 1983).

[19]Karlinsky (1985), 166.

[20]"Poet i Vremia," *Proza,* I, 271.

[21]Joseph Brodsky, *Less Than One: Selected Essays.* (New York: Farrar Straus Giroux, 1986), 195. "Footnote to a Poem" trans. by Barry Rubin.

[22]"Marina's left for zaum. See 'Poem of the Air.' It became crowded for her within the frames of poetry. She is *dolphinlike,* as Shakespeare's Cleopatra says of Antony." Anna Akhmatova, "Tsvetaeva," in *Sochinenia v dvukh tomakh,* (Moscow: Khudozhestvennaiia Litertaura 1986), II, 209.

[23]L.V. Zubova has recently argued that Tsvetaeva's poetry is based on "delineating boundaries" and on "a dialectic or contradiction that finds expression in the potential for multiple meanings of word roots."' *Poezia Mariny Tsvetaevoi: Lingvisticheskii aspekt.* (Leningrad: Leningradskovo Universiteta, 1989), 241–242.

Response to a Questionnaire

Marina Ivanovna TSVETAEVA.
Born September 26, 1892, in Moscow
Aristocrat

Father: A priest's son from the province of Vladimir, a European philologist (his study *Oscan inscriptions* and a series of others), a doctor *honoris causa* of Bologna University, professor of Art History, first at Kiev University, then at Moscow, director of the Rumyantsev Museum, the founder, inspiration, and the only private collector for the first Museum of Fine Arts in Russia (Moscow, Znamenka Street). A Hero of Labour. He died in Moscow in 1913, soon after the opening of the Museum. He left his personal fortune (modest, because he helped others) to a school in Talitsy (Vladmir province, the village where he was born). He gave his own huge library that he acquired with great difficulty to the Rumyantsev Museum, not having removed one book.

Mother: of Polish princely blood, a pupil of Rubinstein, with a rare gift for music. She died young. Poetry is from her.

The library (both her own and my grandfather's) she also gave to the museum. And so from us Tsvetaevs, there are three libraries in Moscow. I would also give my own, if I hadn't had to sell it during the years of the Revolution.

Early childhood: Moscow and Tarusa (a Khlyst enclave on the Oka river),[1] from age 10 to age 13 (the death of my mother) abroad, at age 17 Moscow again. Never lived in the Russian countryside.

Major influence: mother's (music, nature, poems, Germany. A passion for Judaism. One against all. Heroïca). My father's influence more subtle but no less strong. (A passion for work, an absence of careerism, simplicity, aloofness.) Father's and Mother's fused influence: Spartanism. Two leitmotifs in one household: Music and The Museum. At home an atmosphere that was neither bourgeois, nor intellectual: chivalrous. Life on a lofty scale.

Progression of the mind's development: from earliest childhood: music. Age 10: revolution and the sea (Nervi, near Genoa, an emigré enclave). Age 11: Catholicism. Age 12: the first sense of a homeland ("Varangian," Port Arthur).[2] From age 12 on, and even now: Napoleonade, interrupted in 1905 by Spiridonova[3] and Schmidt. Ages 13, 14, 15: populism, collections of the journal *Knowledge,* the dialect of the Don river, Zheleznov's political economy, Tarasov's poetry. Age 16: a break with any idealist or ideological thinking[4], love for Sarah Bernhardt (*The Eaglet*), an outburst of Bonapartism; from ages 16 to 18: Napoleon (Victor Hugo, Béranger, Frédéric Masson, Thiers, memoirs, *Kult*). French and German poets.

First encounter with the Revolution: in 1902–03 (emigrés), the second in 1905–06 (Yalta, the SR's). There was no third.

Sequence of favorite books (each gives an epoch): *Undine* (early childhood), Hauff's *Lichtenschtein* (adolescence). Rostand's *L'Aiglon* (early youth). Later and even now: Heine—Goethe—Hölderlin. Russian prose writers: I'm speaking from my own present temperament: Leskov and Aksakov. Contemporaries: Pasternak. Russian poets: Derzhavin and Nekrasov. Contemporaries: Pasternak.

Most favorite poems in childhood: Pushkin's "To the Sea" and Lermontov's "The Hot Spring." Twofold : "The Forest King" and "Erlkönig." Pushkin's "Gypsies" from age 7 to the present day, to the point of passion. Never liked *Eugene Onegin*.

Favorite books in the world, those to be burned with: *Niebelungen, The Iliad, The Igor Tale.*

Favorite countries: Ancient Greece and Germany.

Education: from age 6: Zograf-Plaksina music school, age 9: girl's gymnasium IV, age 10: none, age 11: Catholic boarding school in Lausanne, age 12: Catholic boarding school in Freiburg (Black Forest), age 13: a gymnasium in Yalta, age 14: Moscow Alfiorova's boarding school, age 16: the Brukhanenko Gymnasium. Finished grade VII, left VIII.

At age 16 attended a summer course in old French literature at the Sorbonne.

The comment on my first French essay (age 11): "Trop d'imagination, trop peu de logique."

I've been writing poems since age 6. Publishing since 16. Have written poetry in both French and German.

First book: *Evening Album.* I published on my own, while still in the gymnasium. The first review: a highly receptive article by Max Voloshin. I don't know the literary influences I know the human.

Favorite writers (of contemporaries): Rilke, R. Rolland, Pasternak. I've been published in journals, in *Severnye Zapiski* (1915), now, abroad, for the most part in *Volya Rossii* , in *Svoimi Putiami* and in *Blagonamerennyi* (the leftist literary flank), and from time to time in *Sovremennye zapiski* (rightist). Because of their deep lack of culture, I'm not published at all by the right wing.

I do not belong to any poetic or political movement and never have.

In Moscow, purely for reasons of daily existence, I became a member of the Writers' Union and, it seems, of the Poets' [A chronological list of her works follows]

Favorite things in the world: music, nature, poems, solitude.

An utter indifference to the public, to the theatre, to the plastic arts, to spectatorship.[5] My sense of ownership is limited to the children and notebooks.

If there were a shield, I'd inscribe: "Ne daigne."
Life is a station, soon I'll depart, where to, I won't say.

Marina Tsvetaeva

Marina Tsvetaeva, *Sochinenija,* ed. Anna Saakjants. (Moscow: Khudozhestvennaiia Literatura, 1988), II, 6–8. Pasternak sent this questionnaire to her in April, 1926. Tsvetaeva changed certain facts, such as her father's being an aristocrat; her mother was a student of one of Rubenstein's pupils.

Notes

[1] A seventeenth century sect of flagellants.

[2] "Varangian;" a ship at the battle of Port Arthur.

[3] Maria Spiridonova, a social revolutionary.

[4] "idealism" suggests a tendentiousness about political ideas or causes, also a Marxist term, for progressive or principled thinking. Here, also art with didactic or social content.

[5] "spectatorship" is a neologism, also the visible.

"Kind reader!"

Kind reader! Laughing like a child,
Cheerfully greet my magic lantern.
Sincere is your laughter, may it be an inexplicable
Ringing, as in the days of old.

All will flit by in the course of an instant;
The knight and the page, magician and king . . .
Away with reflection! For a woman's book
Is only a magic lantern.

(epigraph to *A Magic Lantern*)

"As soon as I close burning eyelids"

As soon as I close burning eyelids—
Paradise roses, paradise rivers . . .

Somewhere afar,
As in a dream-state
The tender words
Of the paradise snake.

And, Sorrowful Eve,
I recognize
The Kingly Tree
In paradise' round.

January 20, 1917

"In a red cluster"

In a red cluster
The rowan tree blazed.
The leaves were falling,
I was born.

Hundreds of bells
Were quarreling.
The day was Saturday:
John the Divine.

Even now
I feel like nibbling at
The fiery rowan's
bitter branch.

August 16, 1916

An Attempt at Jealousy

How's your living with another,
Simpler, really? The stroke of an oar!
Like the line along the shore
Has memory soon receded

About me, a floating island
(In the sky—not in the waters!)
Souls, the souls! may they be
Sisters to you, not lovers!

How's your living with a *simple*
Woman? *Without* the divine?
Now that you've dethroned
Her Majesty (and stepped down),

How is living? Keeping busy?
How is shivering? Getting up?
With the toll of immortal banality
Poor man, how do you cope?

"Convulsions, palpitations—
Cease! I'll rent myself a home."
How is living with just any other
For you, my chosen one?

Is the food more fitting—more
Edible? When you get fed up, don't blame . . .
How is living with a likeness
For you, who's trampled on Sinai!

How's your living with a stranger, local
Woman? Straight to the rib: Is she pleasing?
Doesn't shame with reins of Zeus
Lash against your brow?

How's your living—how's your health?
How are things? How's the singing?
How are you, poor fellow, coping
With immortal conscience' sting?

114

How's your living with wares
From the market? The tariff steep?
After the marbles of Carrara
How's living with the dust of plaster

Of Paris? (Out of rock was hewn
God—and utterly shattered into bits!)
How's your living with the last of a hundred thousand
For you, who's known Lilith?

Sated with the market
Novelty? Cooled to the spell?
How's your living with an earthly
Woman, without the six
Senses?
      So, head in hand: are you happy?
No? In a chasm without depth—
How's your living, darling? Harder,
Or just the same, as mine with another?

November 19, 1924

"In a mist, bluer than incense"

In a mist, bluer than incense,
Paneling—like silver.
To the meeting flies unforetold
A scattered quill.

And now glances already exchanged,
And, with a singer's crack your voice,
Praying for what, shook
The Bohemian crystal.

A moment of sorrow and challenge,
The movement—like a long shout,
And in the waves of the dove-blue mist
Your soft face plunged.

Everything lasted—only an instant.
Set sail . . . Departed . . .
Rival!—I, no less
Wonderful, awaited you!

September 5, 1915

"For a beast"

For a beast—a lair,
For a stranger—the road,
For the dead man—a hearse.
To each his own.

For a woman—to connive,
For a king—to reign,
For me—to praise
Your name.

May 2, 1992
(Poems to Blok)

"I want to force from the mirror"

I want to force from the mirror,
Where there is murk and a misting dream—
Where the path lies for You
And where is the haven.

I see: the mast of a ship,
And You—at the deck . . .
You—in the smoke of a train . . . A field
In the evening plaint . . .

Evening fields in the dew,
Above them—ravens . . .
—I bless You to all
The four regions!

May 3, 1915
(from Woman Friend, *written for Parnok)*

"I'd like to live with You"

I'd like to live with You
In a small town,
Where there are eternal twilights
And eternal bells.
And in a small village inn—
The faint chime
Of ancient clocks—like droplets of time.
And sometimes, in the evenings, from some garret—
A flute,
And the flautist himself in the window.
And big tulips in the window-sills.
And maybe, You would not even love me . . .

In the middle of the room—a huge tiled oven,
On each tile—a small picture:
A rose—a heart—a ship.—
And in the one window—
Snow, snow, snow.

You would lie—thus I love You: idle,
Indifferent, carefree.
Now and then the sharp strike
Of a match.

The cigarette glows and burns down,
And trembles for a long, long time on its edge
In a grey brief pillar—of ash.
You're too lazy even to flick it—
And the whole cigarette flies into the fire.

December 10, 1916

The Window

An Atlantic and delightful
Breath of spring—
A huge butterfly is
My curtain—and—

A Hindu Widow
Into the golden-lipped aperture
A Slumbering Naiad
Into trans-windowed seas...

May 5, 1923

August

August—asters,
August—stars,
August—clusters
Of grapes and rowan
Rust—August!

With your full-weighted, nobly
Inclined imperial apple,
You play like a child, August.
You stroke the heart like a palm
With your imperial name:
August—the Heart!

Month of late kisses,
Late roses and late lightnings!
Of starry torrents—
August!—Month
Of starry torrents!

February 7, 1917

"Life comes not with clamor and thunder"

Life comes not with clamor and thunder,
But so: snow is falling,
Lamps glow, someone's come up
To the house.
The bell blazed—a long spark.
He entered. Gazed.
In the house it's totally quiet.
The icons glow.

1915

"It's time to take off amber"

It's time to take off amber,
It's time to change lexicons,
It's time to put out the lantern
Above the door . . .

February, 1941.

Attempt at a Room

The walls of inertia have been numbered
Before me. But—a leap—Chance?—
I remembered three walls.
I cannot vouch for the fourth.

Well, who knows, back to the wall?
It may **be,** but may well **not**

Be. And never was. It was windy. But
Isn't a wall behind the back? . . . Everything
Not as you like. The dispatch, "Depths,"
The Tsar has abdicated. News not only by

Mail. Urgent wires
From everywhere and everywhen.

Played the piano? There's a draft.
It's blowing. Moves like a sail. Like cotton
Fingers. The sonatina sheet billows.
(Don't forget, you're going on nine).

For that unseen wall
I know the name: the wall of the back

By the piano. Still—beyond the writing
Table, and still further—beyond the shaving

Kit (the wall has a trick—
This one—becomes a corridor

In the mirror. **Transported**—glanced.
(The metaphorical chair of emptiness.)

A chair is for all who don't enter
By the door,—a threshold sensitive to soles!
That wall out of which you've
Grown—pressed on with the past—

Between us there is still a complete
Paragraph. You will appear like D'Anzas—

From behind.
        For **that** one—is like D'Anzas,
Who was summoned, chosen, with time, with weight,
(I know the name: the wall of the spine!)
Enters the room, not as D'Anthes.

A turn of the head. —Ready?
Thus you will too after ten stanzas,

Lines.
        An optic attack in the rear.
But, having abandoned the rank behind-the-back,
The ceiling reliably **was**.
I'm not being stubborn: as in a drawing-room,

It was perhaps a little bit crooked.
(A bayonet attack in the rear—

Of Forces).
        And now already the cerebellum's been
Clamped. The spine sprawled like a clod of earth.
That unbroken wall, the Cheka.
That one—of daybreak, well that one—of shootings

Bright: more distinct than in the shadow of
Gestures—right in the back from behind.

That's what I don't understand: execution.
But, having abandoned the rank from behind-the-wall,
The ceiling reliably was
Whole (still ahead—what's it

To us). I shall return to the fourth wall:
That one there, where, falling back, the coward
Stumbles.
        "Well, what about a floor—
Was there one? Surely one must be on something? . . . "
There was. But not for everyone. For a swing, a trunk,
A horse, a rope, for the sabbath.—

Higher! . . .
        For all of us in **the hereafter**
To fuse emptiness with the point of
Gravity.

A floor is for feet.
—How instilled is man, how interspersed!—
So that there was no dripping—a ceiling.
You remember the old torture—a drop

Every hour? Grass wouldn't grow in the house—
A floor, so that earth wouldn't enter in the house—

Through all these—for whom even a stake
Isn't an obstacle on a May night!
Three walls, a ceiling and a floor.
Everything, it seems? Now then, appear!

Will notify by shutter?
The room was set up hastily,
Whitish on grey—
Sketched in a notebook.

Not the plasterer, not the roofer—
The Dream. On wireless journeys
The Guard. In the Abysses under eyelids
A male has found a female.

Not the purveyor, not the upholsterer—
The Dream, more naked than Revellian
Shallows. A floor without polish.
The Room? It's simply—planes.

A most welcoming landing-stage!
Something out of geometry,
Out of an abyss in a paperback,
Belatedly, but fully understood.

Yet that brake of the phaetons—
The Table? Well, really, a table feeds off of
The elbow. Put the elbow at an inclination,
And it will be the table of tableness.

Just as for children, there are storks:
It will be needed,—and the thing will
Appear. Don't fret from three miles away!
The chair will grow together with the guest.

Everything will grow,
Don't accord, don't build.
Under a shop-sign
Shall I say which?

Of Reciprocity
The Forest's thicket
Hotel
Meeting of Souls

A house for a gathering. All—these
Partings, even for southerners to the south!
Is it hands who are attending?
No, something quieter than hands,

And lighter than hands, and cleaner than
Hands. Renovated rubbish
With complete facilities? Languishment
Left there!

Well, here we are touchy
And rightly so. Heralds of hands,
Ideas—of hands, sums—of hands,
The very ends—of hands . . .

Without any convulsive "where are you's?"
I wait. Kindred to the quiet
They attend—gestures
In Psyche's court.

Only the wind is dear to the poet.
I'm sure of this—in the corridors.

A passage—look, an army base,
You have to go a long way, to come at once

To the middle of the room, in the guise of a God—
Carrying a Lyre . . .
          —The road of verse!—

Wind, wind, above the brow,—like a banner
Raised by our footsteps!

The established "and so forth,"—
Corridors: domesticity of distance.

With a rookish profile of a woman infidel
Distance with a quiet quickness, to the measure of

Children's feet, in a rain-splattered raincoat
Sweet rhymes: slate-pencil,—sandal—

Dutch tile . . . in a peacock-like train
Somewhere there's the tower called Eiffel.

Just as for a child a river—is a pebble,
A division of distance isn't distance, but distancette

In a child's memory, stringed, grounded
Distance with hand luggage, distance like a governess

Not having blurted out to us (distance is in fashion)
Whatever trails along on carts . . .

Distance reduced to a pencil-case . . .
Corridors: canals of houses.

Weddings, destinies, events, dates—
Corridors: tributaries of houses.

At five in the morning, with an anonymous letter,
In the corridor, it's not only brooms that are

Moving. It smells of caraway and turf.
A kind of corporation? Cour-ier-dored!

Only asking that she grind
The corridors—Carmagnole!

Whoever built the corridors
(Dug), knew where to make a bend,
To give the blood time
To turn around the corner

Of the heart—around that acute
Angle—thunder's magnet!
So that the cardiac island
Would be washed on all

Sides. That corridor was created by
Me—don't ask for it to be clearer!
To give the brain time
To notify all along the

Line: from "there's no boarding here"
To the junction of the
Heart: "It's coming! Throw yourself—
Squint! But no—Off

The rails!" That corridor created by
Me, (not the poet—Simply!)
To give the brain time
To assign a place.

For a rendezvous—is an area,
A painting—a calculation,—a sketch—
Of words, not always to the point,
Of gestures, completely in error.

So that love is in order—
Complete, so that it pleases you—
Complete, down to the last fold—
Of lips or a dress? Of a brow.

Everyone knew how to straighten a dress!
Corridors: tunnels of houses.

Just as an old man, led by his daughter,
Corridors: ravines of houses.

My friend, look! As in a letter, as in this dream—
It's I like a ray of light upon you!

In the first dream, when you'll lower your eyelids,
It's I who's upon you like a presentiment

Of light. At the furthest point of time
There I am—a shining eye.

And then what?
There is the dream: in the tone.
There was an ascent
There was an incline

Of a brow—and a brow.
Ahead—Your
Brow. Rough
Rhyme: mouth.

Because no walls remained—
The ceiling reliably keeled

Over. Only the vocative case blossomed
In mouths. While the floor—reliably a gap.

While through the gap, green as the Nile . . .
The ceiling was reliably singing.

The floor—well, what except "Collapse!"
To the floor? What's left for us among the dusty

Floorboards? Too slightly swept?—Higher!
All of the poet by one hyphen

Holds on . . .
                    Above the **nothingness** of two bodies
The ceiling was reliably singing—

Like all the angels.

                    St. Gilles-sur-Vie.
                    June 6, 1926

New Year's Greetings

Happy New Year—new world—region—haven!
The first letter to you in the new
—Misunderstanding, that verdant—
(Verdant—ruminant) place resounding, place resonant
Like the empty tower of Aeolus.
The first letter to you from yesterday's
Motherland, where without you I am longing
Away . . . now already from one of the
Stars . . . The law of exit and retreat,
By which the beloved becomes just anyone
And the unheard of non-existent.
Shall I say how I found out about yours?
Neither by earthquake nor by avalanche.
A man came in—any man—(The beloved—
You). The most sorrowful of events.
In The News and in Days. Will you do an article?
Where? In the mountains. (A window in the pine branches.
A bedsheet.) Don't you see the papers?
What about the article? No. But . . . please spare me.
Aloud: it's hard. Within: won't double-cross.
In a sanatorium. (A paradise for hire.)
—What day?—Yesterday, the day before, I don't remember.
Will you be at the Alcazar?—No.
Aloud: the family. Within: anything, but I'm not Judas.

To the forthcoming one! (That was being born tomorrow!)—
Shall I say what I've done having found out about . . . ?
Tsss . . . A slip of the tongue. Force of habit.
Life and death I've long since put in quotations,
As known-to-be empty fabrications.
I didn't do anything, but something
Was done, something that does without shadow
And echo!

　　　　Now, how did you go?
How was the heart tearing and yet not
Torn?—As if on Orlovian trotters,
Not falling behind, *he said*, Eagles,
It took your breath away—or more?

131

More sweetly? Neither altitude nor descent,
For the one flying on eagles truly
Russian. Our vital tie to the other world:
You spent time in Russia—the other world in this
Beheld. A well-arranged crossing over!
Life and death I pronounce with a grin
Hidden—You will touch it with your own!
Life and death I pronounce with a footnote,
With an asterisk . . . (the night that I long for:
Instead of a cerebral hemisphere—
The starred!)
      Not to forget, my friend,
The following: that if Russian
Letters were to take the place of German—
It's not because now, so they say,
All will pass, that a dead man (destitute) will eat all—
Not batting an eye!—but because that *other* world,
Ours—at thirteen, at Novodevochy
I understood: is not without, but all-tongued.

And so I'm asking, not without sorrow:
You no longer ask, what's the Russian for
"Nest"? The only and all-nests
Covering rhyme: star-celest.

Am I digressing? But no such thing
Will be found,—to digress away from you.
Each and every thought, Du Lieber, any
Syllable leads to you—no matter
The sense. . . (let German be more native than Russian for
Me, the angelic most native of all!)—just as there is no place
Where you are not, no "there is": the grave.
Everything as it wasn't and as it was.
Is there really nothing at all about me?
The surroundings, Rainer, your overall condition?
Urgently, without fail—
The first vision of the universe,
It's implied, of the poet
In the latter) and the last—of the planet,
Given once only to you—in its wholeness!

Not poet and ashes, not spirit and body,
(To separate is to offend both)
But you with yourself again, you with you,
Being like Zeus doesn't mean being the best—
You—Castor, with yourself—Pollux,
You marble, with yourself,—grass,
Not a parting and not a meeting—an eye-to-eye
Encounter: both the first meeting and
Parting.
    How you glanced at your
Hand (at the trace—of ink—on it)
From your own so-many (how many) miled
Without end for without beginning
Height above the crystal level
Of the Mediterranean—and other discs.
Everything as it wasn't and how everything will be
Also for me beyond the end of the suburb.
Everything as it wasn't and everything as it is already
—For someone who's corresponded, what's a spare
Week!—and wherever *else* is there to look,
Leaning on the rim of the loge,
From this one,—if not at that one, from that one
If not at this long-suffering one.
I live in Bellevue. A town of nests and
Branches. Exchanged glances with a guide:
Bellevue. A gaol with a wonderful view
Of Paris—The mansion of a gallic chimera—
Of Paris—and on a bit further . . .
Leaning on the scarlet rim
How amusing they are for you (for whom) "it must be,"
(Yet for me) They *must* be, from a height without measure,
Our Bellevue and Belvederes!

I'm shifting tack . . . Particularity. Immediacy.
New Year's on the threshold. What for, with whom will I clink
   glasses
Across the table? With what? Instead of bubbles—a shred
Of cotton. Why? Well, it strikes—but what's it to me?
What am I to do in the New Year's noise
With the internal rhyme: Rainer died.
If you, such an eye, could darken,
It means life is not life, death is not death.
It means, it's getting dark, I'll understand it all when we meet!—

133

There is neither life nor death, there is the third,
The New. And behind it (The seventh is
Covered with straw, the twenty-sixth
Is passing, what happiness
To end and begin with you!)
Across the table, beyond the grasp of the eye,
You and I will toast with a quiet clink
Of glass against glass? No, not with their tavernish:
You an' I, flowing together giving the rhyme:
The Third.
   Across the table I look at your cross.
Such space out of town, so many places
Beyond the city! And to whom does the shrub
Wave, if not to us? How many places—namely ours
And no one else's! All the foliage! The entire pine-branch!
Your places with me (yours with yourself).
(Should I say that with you I'd even go to a rally)—
Why mention places! What about months as well!
And weeks! And rainy suburbs
Without people! And mornings! And everything together
Not even begun by nightingales!

I really see poorly, for I'm in a ditch,
You really see better, from on high:
Nothing came of us.
To such a point, so purely and so simply
Nothing, so up to it and ready were
We—that there's no need to elaborate.
Nothing, except, don't expect anything
Out of line, (whoever's out of step
Is wrong), but in line with what,
And how should it be?
   An eternal refrain:
There is nothing that might somehow hint at something
Anything, even from afar, not even a shadow's
Shadow. No matter what hour, what day,
What house, even a condemned man in stocks
Has what memory gave: that mouth!
Or have we probed the means too much?
Out of all *this* only that *other* world
Was ours, as we ourselves are only a reflection
Of us,—instead of all of this one, the entire *other* world!

To the least built up of outskirts—
To the new place, Rainer, to the new world, Rainer!
To the extreme promontory of proof—
To the new eye, Rainer, to new hearing, Rainer!

Everything for you was
A Hindrance: passion and friend.
To the new sound, Echo!
To the new echo, Sound!

How many times at the school-desk:
What mountains are there? What rivers?
Good landscapes without tourists?
Was I mistaken, Rainer, is paradise mountainous,
Thunderous? Not widows' claims,
Really not just one paradise, above it another
Paradise? Terraced? I'm judging by the Tatras.
Paradise cannot not be an amphitheatre.
(Yet the curtain's been lowered above someone . . .)
I wasn't mistaken, Rainer. God—*growing*
Baobab? Not the Sun-King Louis,
Not really just one God? Above him there's really another
God?

How's the writing going in the new place?
However, where *there is* you, *there is* verse: you yourself are
Verse! How's the writing in the good old life
Without a table for your elbow, a brow for your wrist
(A handful).
News received in the usual code!
Rainer, do you enjoy new rhymes?
For interpreting correctly the word
Rhyme what is Death if not a whole new
Series of rhymes?
Nowhere to go: language learned.
A complete row of meanings and consonances
Of the New.

Until we meet again! Until our acquaintance!
We'll see each other; I don't know, but we'll be in tune.
To a land unknown to myself,
To the entire sea, Rainer! To my entire self!

So as not to part ways, drop me a line in time.
To the new sound's design, Rainer!

In the sky there's a ladder with Gifts . . .
To the new placing of hands, Rainer!

So it isn't spilled on, I hold it in my palm,
Above the Rhone and above the Rarogne,
Above apparent and impenetrable separation,
Into Rainer—Maria—Rilke's—hands.

Bellevue, February 7, 1927

Sophia Parnok
(1885–1933)

" . . . I haven't forgotten, you see, in this life, . . . what
   my women friends sang in antiquity in the school
   of Sappho. "

When Sophia Parnok died in 1933, there were so many mourners
at her horse-drawn funeral procession that the streets of Moscow
had to be closed to transport and the Writers' Union, then the Herzen
House, held a reception to honor her. Though prominent in the literary circles of the 1910s and 1920s, she has mostly been known
since for her affair with Tsvetaeva from October 1914 to February
1916. In her lifetime she was an accomplished poet, author of
children's stories, and, under the pseudonym of A. Polyanin, a critic
and translator of Baudelaire, Paul Roux, Proust, Giraudoux, and
others.

Sophia Parnok was born in Taganrog to a well-to-do Jewish family.[1] As Sophia Poliakova points out, Parnok started to write poetry
as a child, and was a rather rebellious and intellectual young girl.
"In the eyes of my father, I am a wild kid, and nothing else. My way
of thinking and tastes wound his patriarchal virtues, and he conde-
scends to me."[2] After graduating from a gymnasium, she went off to
Geneva, where she lived with the Plekhanovs and studied in a music
conservatory. Though she quit the school and returned to Russia,
music remained a central concern for her. Her collection "Music"
was published in 1926. Parnok also wrote opera librettos. Her legend "Almast" was staged to successful reviews in a branch of the
Bolshoi Theatre in the summer of 1930, with Molotov and Stalin
rumored to be in the audience.

After her return to Russia, Parnok, like Akhmatova, studied law.
Although she had wanted to apply to the historical-philological department, she chose law because this was a more viable option for
women who wanted a higher education. Apparently she did not complete her law studies.

Her brief marriage to the critic Volkenstein was not a success for
Parnok the woman, who was always an avowed lesbian, like her
contemporary Allegro. But it proved beneficial to Parnok the writer,
since she began to publish a lot of her poetry after she met him; her
first collection of poetry appeared when she was twenty-one.

As a pacifist and convert to Russian Orthodoxy, Parnok was deeply affected by World War I and the Revolution. Her world view was informed by Christian and Slavophile ideas. In her categorical rejection of the Bolshevik Revolution, she shares the same perspective as Akhmatova, Gippius, and Tsvetaeva. In the Crimea, Parnok became involved with a group of artists, painters, and actresses at Sudak; she was a central figure at Max Voloshin's famous artistic haven in Koktebel, which was a thriving artists' community despite the hardships of civil war. Their dire material situation prompted Tsvetaeva and Parnok's former husband Volkenstein to go to Lunacharsky in Moscow to ask for assistance on their behalf. Parnok was later to refer to Sudak, where she wrote *Roses of Pieria*, as "the homeland of her youth."

In 1922, Parnok returned to Moscow, and became involved in the literary salons, published collections, and joined the group "The Lyrical Circle." Here she also became more involved in the literary and editorial work of the journal *Bundle* (*Yzel*), a cooperative venture which she had helped found. Since it became increasingly difficult to finance the journal, and to publish poetry, it was dissolved in 1928.

Parnok's poetry is distinguished by its formal simplicity and clarity.[3] Russian writers who influenced her most were Tiuchev, Baratynsky, and Pavlova. Orthodox religious motifs recur in her poetry, and like Akhmatova, she was accused of religiosity. In the *Literary Encyclopedia* of 1934, her work is characterized as filled with a constant repetition "of the symbols and attributes of the Christian cult."

Parnok's poetry also celebrates womanhood, a mythic female heroism; Eve, Sybil, Pensefeleia, the amazon queen, and others figure in her poetry, and many of her themes are gender-defined. Her status as an accomplished woman poet and avowed lesbian attests to the relatively tolerant social climate of Russia at the time prior to the Bolshevik concentration of power.[4] Conscious of Sappho as precursor, Parnok echoes the poet whom in her cycle *The Roses of Pyreia* she called the tenth muse, adding this note to an idea of woman's empowerment through poetry.

Notes

[1]Her father was a pharmacist and managed a drugstore. Her mother, Alexandra Abramovna Idelson, was a physician who died from complications after the birth of Parnok's twin brother and sister. Her father then married the German governess. Parnok took pride in her Jewish heritage and the Judaic figures in her poetry as it does in Tsvetaeva's. In "For the Jews," an early lyric, she wrote:

"Let oppressions, humiliations,/Strengthen the centuries old subjugation/They hasten awakening,/And the Jewish spirit shall be enlivened./It shall live, it shall quiver,/It shall rouse everyone/And then,/Above the dark abyss shall shine/The star that has now died down."(Polyakova, 19).

[2]Poliakova, 8.

[3]To Briusov, her experimentation with classical meters gave her poetry an artificial rhythm and fragmented quality. As S. Poliakova points out, Parnok also uses everyday language in a manner highly unusual for formal poetry.

[4]Simon Karlinsky points out that the pre-revolutionary climate was far more tolerant than during the later Bolshevik period. Many writers were openly homosexual. Rozanov wrote a defense of Oscar Wilde; the symbolist Kliuev was gay; Kuzmin published his autobiographical *Wings* in 1905, later banned by the Bolsheviks.(Karlinsky, 1985, 53).

"Yet somewhere there are cool rivers"

Yet somewhere there are cool rivers
and neither the cursed nor the kind,
and one sky above all.

And each word is forever,
and wondrously singing in the veins
the heavenly wine ripens.

And the eternal spinning-wheel of Coolness
soundlessly from the dense mountain ridge
spins the waterfall's thread.

And icon-lamps give light,
the kind that even the devil
cannot melt into gold coins.

(1922)

"On the luxuriant chestnut trees you light"

On the luxuriant chestnut trees you light
wedding candles again, spring.
I tune the soul as in olden days,
to sing songs, but they only ring out
lullabies and dirges,
The consolers of a dream.

"Half-spring and half-autumn!"

Half-spring and half-autumn!
In the break of murky clouds
A pensive blue tint swims,
In the moist distances a violet forest.

Pressed by the wind to the wayside
The ore of an autumn leaf,
And the cold comes on time with a tremble
Along the chilly quiet of the pond.

But will the heat not burst in this sky?
In the foliage of these groves?
Already the young stem turns green
In the grasses' gray streaks of summers past.

"In blue: the dark-rose sunset"

In blue: the dark-rose sunset
and a woman, the kind of whom poets sing.
The evening wind fans her shawl:
in the deep blue, crimson bouquets.

And a smoothness of shoulders and sharpness of elbows
the patterned cloth has revealed, flooded back.
Transparent almonds of fingernails
more festive than pearls and rubies.

Young women martyrs have such brows
and hair, more still than a crown.
Under the arc of a maidenly upper lip
already a more tender outlined abundance.

What kind of artist sketched this brow,
and on the temple touched the azure vein,
where more of Rurik's Varangian blood
has mixed with the glorious blood of Comnena.*

*Alexius I (1081–1118), Byzantine emperor, whose daughter Anna Comnena
  was a historian of great importance.

Sapphic Strophes

Too taut were the lips clenched.
Could the word pass through there?
But your voice summoned me—I listen
with a tender name.

Yet when, so close and again strange,
we have returned, above midnight Moscow
the wind has rushed from distant shores,
the sea wind blew.

Wind, wind from the sea, my one avenger
will fly in again, so that you, lamenting,
will remember the hour, when with my lips
I listened to your heart.

"He goes with a radiant woman"

He goes with a radiant woman
—They told me,—
My house open to all the winds,
all the winds.

They are music lovers—
At nine in the Kursaal,
Her figure is slender,
so slender ...

I see: the misty shore,
at the twilight hour,
the shore, hills and heather,
and heather.

And next to broad felt
white feathers ...
A heart open to all the winds,
all the winds!

17 June, 1915.

"You appeared before me like a clumsy little girl."
Sappho

"You appeared before me like a clumsy little girl."
Ah, Sappho's arrow has pierced me with one line of verse.
At night, lost in thought, above the curly small head,
replacing a mad heart's passion with a mother's tenderness—
"You appeared before me like a clumsy little girl."

I remembered, how you dismissed a kiss with a trick,
remembered those eyes with remarkable pupils ...
You entered my home, happy with me, as with something new:
A belt, handfuls of beads or colorful boots,—
"You appeared before me like a clumsy little girl."

But under strokes of love you are malleable gold!
I bowed to your face, pale in the ardent shadow,
where it is as if death passed over like a snowy feather ...
I thank you, my delightful one, because in those days
"You appeared before me like a clumsy little girl."

February 1915
(Written for Tsvetaeva.)

"And the curtain has opened"

And the curtain has opened
and I gaze, gaze
at the first snow, at newly
blossomed dawn.
At the rose cloud,
at the pale blue shade,
at this bettered day
in a new form.
Like a small glass bell
the forest's quiet resounds,
and in the pine-needled forest you
stand subdued.

"So illusively and so clearly"

So illusively and so clearly
Did I recall this long noon,
both the vineyard, and the windmill
winged in the depth of the valley.

And the shadow turned like a wheel
along the curled dale,
and that glass day was for me,
like a day in paradise, singing and long ...

And then I go into the quiet
and recognize both light and shadow,
and the homeland of my soul
I welcome with a heartbeat.

A sloping descent. And a turn.
And three steps to the reservoir,
and then, wanderess, and then
you and I finally are home.

1927

Anna Akhmatova
(1889–1966)

As few poets have done, Anna Akhmatova (1889–1966) both lived and reflected in her poetry a quintessentially exemplary Russian woman's life.[1] This situation, as much as her modernist associations, provides a ground for her poetry, which is autobiographical in ways that popular poetry often is. Deeply intuitive in its enlistment of image and sequence, it remains unusually conservative, and in its last expressions uncertain, for the work of so important a poet.

In her life Akhmatova ran the course from the lively *dyevushka,* the seductively appealing and gifted girl or ingénue, to the deeply sorrowing *babushka,* the sad-faced and bountifully kindly grandmother. As a *dyevushka* she met her first husband, Nikolai Gumilyev, when she was barely fourteen and married him at twenty. With and through him she began publishing in her teens, became one of the most celebrated poets in Russia by the time she was twenty-five, lived the artistic life at places like the "Wandering Dog" Café, and festively travelled abroad, where she befriended Modigliani and savored the excitements of nascent modernism. She lived in the thick of poetic projects and amorous intrigues, great poet and *femme fatale* all in one, a star.

But the shadow of suffering fell early with the execution of Gumilyev, in 1921. This haunted her even though by then they were already divorced. And as a *babushka* she was to continue suffering, through the long ban on her work, lifted only intermittently the rest of her life until her last years. In her personal life, the sufferings were equally protracted: her only son served two heavy sentences in a prison camp. To the oppressions of the war—the bombings of Leningrad, exile in Tashkent—were added the torturing uncertainties of a helpless mother. And then later, after her son's second long sentence was finally over, he showed her the troubled evasiveness that is typical of modern sons. Moreover, through the quarter century during which she became a *babushka,* she lived in the atmosphere described by Nadezhda Mandelshtam, the terror that brought Mandelshtam and others to sudden arrest and horrible death. For the celebrated national figure and generous literary sponsor she became in her last years the sufferings remained a resonant and validating undertone.

In stanzas more resoundingly classic than any of her American contemporaries Sara Teasdale and Edna St. Vincent Millay, the *dyevushka* brought to nearly proverbial expression the many ins and outs of her love life. Later, in popular poems, the *babushka* celebrated

149

her patriotism, and the devastations of war. She expanded on her own personal devastations in three long poems: *Requiem,* which lists a stark, even crude, series of sorrowful blows; *The Way of All the Earth,* which recounts sorrows in the *persona* of a legendary *babushka;* and *Poem Without a Hero,* which resurrects the rococo or *Art Nouveau* note of her youthful milieu to invoke a ghost and run through a panorama of sorrowful remembrances. It is impossible to read these poems without some recognition of what their writer has suffered.

Fortunately that voice was not quelled. The *babushka* brought it all together in several poems, the joys of the *dyevushka* as they merge and transfuse into the later sufferings, and most notably in the *Northern Elegies.* This sequence of six meditative poems, to use English comparisons, strikes a register somewhere between Tennyson and T.S. Eliot.

The poems of the legendary *dyevushka,* too, need sorting; the charm of a female Byron must be resisted, as for the later poems we must assess what is poetic and what simply evocative in the solemn piety they command. Still, their charm and their solemnity, at this poet's best, fuse fully in the high ring of the revelatory and the inevitable.

The restrained simplicity that Akhmatova distills in her poems derives from the style of Pushkin and his successors. Her steady and composed understatement keeps her vein closer to the romantic one than to the vein of those with whom she was personally associated among her contemporaries. Reading her poems by themselves, and particularly her early, limpid ones, we would never link her to her fellow "Acmeists" Gumilyev and Mandelshtam, though as Sam Driver points out in his book on Akhmatova, her economy of image and her indirectness of presentation can be derived from their program. Still, there is little in her style that fulfills the modernist aspirations of the Acmeists, other than an austere economy of expression. Gumilyev is somewhat more abstract, Mandelshtam considerably more. Still less does she match the iconoclastic stridency of Mayakovsky, or the deeply structured if muted involutions of Pasternak, though in "Boris Pasternak" she does imitate his kind of image formation.

All these poets abjured the Symbolists, but even Balmont and Blok exhibit a more programmatic modernism than Akhmatova. They break more definitely with the line of Pushkin, Tiutchev, and Nekrasov. Balmont and Blok invent a more saturated version of the Verlaine whom Akhmatova and Modigliani recited to each other, but whose metaphoric coherences she never strongly adopted. Some of the qualities of her style can be derived from the delicacy aimed at in *Art Nouveau,* as Alexis Rannit has shown (in an essay prefac-

ing the second volume of her Collected Works). Yet, finally, she derives far more firmly from the classic simplicities achieved for Russian style by Pushkin. Akhmatova's resolute understatement markedly matches Pushkin's, a poet whose work occupies the bulk of her
small critical-scholarly output. Understatement is the tonic note, indeed, for the long tradition she epitomizes, a note most clearly
sounded in English by the poetry of Robert Frost (a poet she happened to meet at a long ceremonial luncheon during her last years).
Other analogues would be hard to find in our century; perhaps the
Pavese of *Lavorare Stanca* for the *Northern Elegies*. To match those
late meditative blank verse poems we would do better, again, to look
to an earlier time for more appropriate analogues—-to Wordsworth
or Foscolo, Musset or Mörike. And at the same time early poems
like "A Drive", ringing rhymes and all, are in touch with a spirit of
sensitive amorous reflection not wholly different from what may be
found in the lyrics of Cole Porter or the blues, a similarity that would
help explain her great, rapid popularity.

The sequence "In Tsarskoe Selo" neatly surveys through muted
detail a place of reality and legend shared by both Akhmatova and
Pushkin. She grew up there, he attended the *lycée* during the years
of his formation as a poet.

The seriality—what some would call the metonymy—of
Akhmatova's images is abundantly clear in "He loved three things in
the world," where each image is drenched with association:

> He loved three things in the world:
> Singing at vespers, white peacocks,
> And blurred maps of America.
> He did not love it when children cried,
> Did not love tea with raspberry jam
> And feminine hysterics.
> . . . But I was his wife.

Singing at vespers, white peacocks, and blurred maps of America
form no order. Nor do crying children, raspberry jam taken with
tea, and feminine hysterics, except as items in a domestic scene with
the tea compensating for the other two. Nor does the second triad
firmly contrast with items in the first. "But I was his wife," the last
line, will cover assuredly the second triad; since the speaker is a poet,
it can be made to cover the first triad also. And still the series is
random, because neither romantic reactions nor domesticity include
the central, complex interaction between male and female. As she
says in "Nothing to me are the ode's ranks", a single detail suffices
to begin the poetic evocation, followed by another detail, "An angry
screech, smell of fresh tar,/ Mysterious mould on a wall/ And the
verse already sounds, fervid, tender,/ A joy for you and for me."

Symbol, though, remains an intermittent possibility, often a climactic one. The poet may have sudden recourse at the end of a poem to a symbolic set that at once lifts the poem's level of figuration and performs an act of closure upon it:

Under the frozen roof of the empty dwelling
I do not count the deadly days;
I read the Apostles' messages,
The words of the Psalmist do I read.
But the stars are blue, frost is fluffy.
Each meeting's more wonderful;
And in the Bible a red maple leaf
Is placed at the Song of Songs.

A somewhat schematized love relation, at once arduous and fulfilling, is presented through a sequence of images that are themselves fairly conventional for the Russian poet, their modernity evidenced only in the stepping up of the traditional Russian understatement. In tone, and also in situation, this poem resembles Tiutchev, except that the speaker refrains austerely from commentary. The dwelling is empty, and yet there are wonderful meetings. The speaker finds the days so deadly she cannot count them, and she both compensates and rises to a new level by reading the Old and the New Testaments. Color comes only in line four, blue stars and fluffy frost. It matches the wonder of the meetings in this winter that contains within itself, finally, not just the emptiness of the first line but the fullness of the last. The red maple leaf used as a place marker for the Bible's one love poem evokes the seasonal cycle, and also the summer of the Biblical poem, otherwise not mentioned. The single color of the leaf holds, signifies, marks a place, and serves synecdochically for the course of the seasons, preserving the peak of autumn in the dead of winter. It also serves metaphorically for the live, though strained, love for which the Song of Songs is at once a definer and a mouthpiece, superseding and presumably including the Gospels and the Psalms, as the leaf includes the year and the year echoes the urges and fruitions of the lovers. This entire metaphorical system is moderately classical; only the compacting into this simplicity is unclassical in its modified modernity.

The manipulation of understatement by the mutings of a terminal image, the preservation of an air of open signification by the evasion of interlocking metaphors—these strengths are adopted for the discursive style of the *Northern Elegies,* which easily flow in and out of something akin to surrealism. In these masterly poems the revelatory detail and the summary reflection conjoin for a deep harmony:

And in Staraya Russa there are splendid gutters,
And in little gardens rotting pergolas,
And the glass of windows as dark as an ice hole . . .

As though all things which I within myself
All my life struggled with, had gained a life,
A separate one, and were embodied in these
Blind walls, in this dark garden . . .

The laugh has still not died, the tears are streaming,
The inkstain darkened, not rubbed off of the table,
And like print upon the heart, there is a kiss—
The only one, in farewell, not to be forgotten . . .

The vision of the poem transmutes the "epochs of remembrances," gathering up the kiss "like print upon the heart" for a meditative calm so all-embracing it can assimilate amorous transports at one end and harrowing troubles at the other. Understatement, direct statement, and the dexterities of near-hyperbole, here merge in a single, unique style.

[1]A longer version of this essay appears as "The Modified Modernism of Anna Akhmatova" in *Soundings* (Detroit: Wayne University Press, 1991).

Northern Elegies

All is in sacrifice to your memory

Pushkin

I
Prehistory

I now live elsewhere

Pushkin

The Russia of Dostoevsky. A moon
Almost at the quarter covered by a bell-tower.
Bars are doing business, cabs are flying.
Five-story buildings are springing up
On Gorokhovaya Street, at Znamenya, near Smolni.
Everywhere there are dancing schools, money-changers' signs.
Next door, coiffeurs: "Henriette," "Basile," "André"
And splendid coffins for sale: " Shumilov Senior."
But anyway, the city has little changed.
Not I alone but also others
Have noticed that it sometimes has the power
Of looking like an old lithograph,
Not a first-class one, but one quite decent,
From, it would seem, the eighteen-seventies.
       Especially a winter before dawn
       Or at twilight.—Then outside the gates
       The harsh, straight Liteini Prospect darkens,
       Not yet put to disgrace by the Modern,
       And vis-à-vis my home Nekrasov lives
       And Saltikov . . . Both of them on a tablet
       Of memorial. O how fearful it would be
       For them to see these tablets! I pass on.
In Staraya Russa there are splendid gutters,*
And in little gardens rotting pergolas,
And the glass of windows as dark as an ice hole,
And it seems so much has happened there
That it is better not to look; let's go away.
Not in every place can an arrangement be made

So that it might open up its secret.
(And in Optina I shall be no more . . .).

The rustling of skirts, checkered plaids,
Frames of walnut wood around mirrors
That are wonder-struck by a Karenin beauty,
And in narrow corridors those wallpapers
With which we were enamoured in childhood,
Under a yellow kerosene lamp
And the same plush on the armchairs . . .
        Everything egghead, slapdash, no matter how . . .
        Fathers and misunderstood grandfathers. The lands
        Mortgaged. And in Baden—the roulette.

And a woman with transparent eyes
(Of so deep a blue that you could not
Not remember the sea looking into them),
With a most uncommon name and a white little hand
And a kindness that for a legacy
I, as it may be, received from her—
A needless gift in my cruel life . . .

The country shivers, but the Omsk convict**
Understood it all, put a cross on it all.
See, now he mixes it all up,
And he himself, at the primeval chaos,
Like some spirit soars away. Midnight strikes.
The pen is creaking on and many pages
Are redolent of the Semenovsky drill field.

This is when we got the idea of being born;
And, unerringly measuring time,
So nothing would be left out of the mysterious
Sights, we said goodbye to non-existence.

*Dostoevsky's retreat, original of the village in *The Brothers Karamazov.*

**Dostoevski.

155

II

And in no way was it a rosy childhood . . .
Of little freckles and teddy bears and toys,
And kind aunts, and fearful uncles, and even
Friends among the pebbles of the river.
As for myself, I began from the start
To see myself as someone's dream or delirium
Or another's reflection in a mirror
Without a name, without flesh, without a cause.
I already knew the list of crimes
That I was obligated to commit.
And here I was, stepping out, a sleepwalker;
I stepped into life and life frightened me.
It spread out before me as the meadow
Where long ago Proserpina took her stroll.
Before me, without kin, clumsy as I was
The unexpected doors opened up.
And people issued forth and cried out
"She has arrived, she has arrived herself!"
I looked at them with consternation
And I thought, "These people have gone mad!"
And the more strongly they gave me praise,
The more strongly the people delighted in me,
The more fearful it was for me to live in the world;
And the more strongly I wanted to awaken,
I knew I would pay a hundredfold
In prison, in the tomb, in the insane asylum,
Everywhere it is decreed for such as me
To wake up—but the torture of happiness endured.

III

In that house it was very fearful to live,
And not the shine of the patriarchal fireside,
Not the little cradle of my son,
Not the fact that both of us were young
And full of intimations
Lessened this feeling of terror.
And I learned how to laugh at all that
And I set out a little bit of wine
And a morsel of bread for whoever at night
Like a dog might scratch at the door
Or took a look into the lower window,
At the time when we, staying still, were trying
Not to see what was going on behind the mirror,
Under whose paces growing ponderous
The steps upon the murky staircase groaned
As though praying for mercy piteously.
And you said, smiling in a strange way,
"Whom on the staircase are 'they' taking away?"

Now you are there where they know all, tell us:

What was living in this house besides ourselves?

IV

Here it is just so—this autumn landscape
Which I have been so afraid of all my life:
And the sky—like an abyss ablaze,
And the city's sounds, as if from the other world
They had been heard, alien forever.
As though all things which I within myself
All my life struggled with, had gained a life,
A separate one, and were embodied in these
Blind walls, in this dark garden . . .
But at this very moment at my shoulder
My former house has still been following me
With a squinting, unfavorable eye,
That window I have always in my memory.
Fifteen years—and it is as though they simulated
Fifteen centuries made of granite,
But I myself have been as though of granite:
Now say a prayer, torment yourself, call me
The queen of the sea. It's all the same. No need . . .
There was a need to convince myself
That all of this has happened many times
And not with me alone—with others also—
And even worse. No, not worse—better.
And my voice—this, it is true, was
Most frighteningly of all said out of the dark:
"Fifteen years ago with such a song
You met this day; you prayed for heaven,
For choruses of stars, and choruses of waters
That they might welcome a triumphal meeting
With him from whom today you have gone away . . .

Here it is just so, your silver wedding:
Well then, summon guests, rejoice, triumph!"

V

Me, like a river,
This stern epoch has turned aside.
They replaced my life. In another channel
It has flowed on past another place,
And I do not recognize my own shores.
O how many sights I have let slip,
And the curtain will have gone up without me
And fallen the same way. How many of my friends
I did not meet in my life a single time,
And how many cities in their outlines
Might have elicited tears from my eyes,
But I know just one city in the world
And by groping I could find it in my sleep.
How many verses I have not written,
And their secret chorus wanders round me
And, it may even be that at some time
They will strangle me . . .
The beginnings and the ends are known to me
And life after the end, and something else,
Of which I need not now make recollection.
And there is some woman or other who has
Occupied my own singular place;
She carries my most lawful proper name,
Leaving for me a nickname out of which
I have done, if you please, all that I could.
I will not, alas, lie in my own tomb.

But sometimes the crazy wind of spring
Or the combination of words in a random book
Or someone's smile will suddenly draw me
Into a life that never came about.
In such a year such and such would have happened,
But in this one—this: to travel, to see, to think,
To recollect, and into a new love
To enter, as into a mirror, with numb awareness
Of betrayal, and of something not there yesterday,
A wrinkle.

But if from there I had taken a look back
At my own life as it is today,
I would have learned what envy is at last.

VI

There are three epochs for remembrances.
And the first as though the day of yesterday.
The soul is underneath their blessed vault,
And the body is in bliss under their shadow.
The laugh has still not died, the tears are streaming,
The inkstain darkened, not rubbed off of the table;
And like print upon the heart, there is a kiss—
The only one, in farewell, not to be forgotten,
But it does not keep going on for long . . .
Already no vault is over the head, but somewhere
In the remote suburbs is a solitary house,
Where in winter it is cold, but hot in summer,
Where there are spiders, dust lies on everything,
Where flaming letters are reduced to ash
And the portraits are changing stealthily,
Whither, as to a tomb, the people go,
And on returning wash their hands with soap
And shake a superficial teardrop off
From tired eyelids and sigh heavily . . .
But the clock is ticking on, one spring
Changes for another, the sky goes pink,
The names of the cities are changing,
Already there are no witnesses to events,
And none with whom to weep, none to remember.
And slowly the shadows go away from us,
Which we are no longer summoning,
And we'd be terrified by their return.
And, once we wake up, we see we have forgotten
Even the path to the solitary house
And, stifling out of shame and vexation,
We run there, but (as it happens in a dream)
There all is other: the people, the things, the walls,
And nobody knows us—we are strangers!
We have landed in the wrong place—my God!
And now when something bitterer arrives:
We realize that we cannot make room
For that past in the boundary of our lives,

And to us it is almost as alien,
As to our neighbor in the apartment next door.
That those who died we would not recognize
And those from whom God sent us separation
Manage beautifully without us—and even
All is for the better . . .

And the heart, already it does not respond,
But my voice, exulting and sorrowing,
All is over . . . and my song is carried
In the waste night, where there's nothing more of you.

(1943–1955)

"All promised him to me"

All promised him to me:
The sky's edge, dim and heart-red,
And a dear dream at Christmas,
And Easter's much-sounding wind,

And the crimson withes of vines,
And the park waterfalls,
And two big dragonflies
On the rusted iron fence.

And I could not fail to believe,
That he would be friends with me,
When on the hill slopes I walked,
Along the hot stone path.

In Tsarskoe Selo
(to Pushkin)
I

Down the alley they are leading horses.
Long are the waves of the carded manes.
O captivating town of riddles,
I am sad, having fallen in love with you.

Strange to remember: my soul was gloomy
Sighing in a mortal delirium.
But now I have become a little plaything
Like my rosy friend the cockatoo.

My breast is not squeezed to pain by foreboding.
If you wish, look into my eyes.
I do not love just the hour before sunset,
A wind from the sea, and the word "Depart."

II

But there is my marble double
Thrown down beneath the old maple;
To the lake waters he gave his face,
He listens to the green rustle.

And shiny rains are dampening
His wound that is clotted with gore . . .
Cold, white as you are, wait;
I too will become marble.

III

A dark youth wanders along the alleys
Beside the remote shores of the lake.
And for a hundred years we have cherished
The stir of his steps, barely audible.

The needles of the pines, thick and prickly,
Have covered the low stumps over . . .
Here lay his three-cornered hat
And a dog-eared volume of Parny.

"Nothing to me are the ode's ranks"

Nothing to me are the ode's ranks
And the charm of the elegy's passion.
In my verse all must be out of place
And not as folk would have it.

If you only knew from what trash
Verses grow, that know no shame,
Like a yellow dandelion at a fence,
Like burdock or the swan's foot plant.

An angry screech, smell of fresh tar,
Mysterious mould on a wall
And the verse already sounds, fervid, tender,
A joy for you and for me.

"Under the frozen roof of the empty dwelling"

Under the frozen roof of the empty dwelling
I do not count the deadly days,
I read the Apostles' messages,
The words of the Psalmist do I read.
But the stars are blue, but frost is fluffy,
And each meeting's more wonderful,
And in the Bible a red maple leaf
Is placed at the Song of Songs.

"There is in the closeness of people a hidden line"

There is in the closeness of people a hidden line,
Infatuations and passions cannot cross it,—
Though in the eerie silence lips flow together,
And hearts are torn to pieces by love.

And friendship here is powerless, and years
Of lofty and fiery happiness,
When the soul is free and alien
To the sluggish languor of voluptuousness.

Those who strive toward it are senseless, and those
Who attain to it are stricken down by gloom . . .
Now you have understood the reason why
My heart will not beat beneath your hand.

A Drive

The plume brushed on the carriage roof.
I glanced into his eyes.
The heart pined, not even knowing
The causes of its grief.

An evening windless and in sorrow bound
Beneath the dome of cloudy skies,
And as though sketched with India ink
In an old album is the Bois de Boulogne.

A smell of benzine and of lilac,
A peace that holds itself on the alert—
He has touched my knees anew
With a hand that is almost not atremble.

Parting

Nocturnal and sloping
Before me is the path.
Just yesterday, in love,
He prayed: "Do not forget."
And now there are only winds,
And the cries of shepherds,
Cedars in turbulence
Around the clean springs.

"He loved three things in the world"

He loved three things in the world:
Singing at vespers, white peacocks,
And blurred maps of America.
He did not love it when children cried,
Did not love tea with raspberry jam
And feminine hysterics.
. . . But I was his wife.

"Like a white stone in a deep well"

Like a white stone in a deep well
There lies in me a single memory.
I cannot and I do not want to struggle.
It is delight and it is suffering.

It seems to me that whoever closely looked
Into my eyes would see it at a stroke.
He would become sadder and more pensive
Than one listening to a mournful tale.

I am sure that the gods used to turn
People into objects and not kill consciousness.
So that forever wondrous griefs would live,
You are turned into my memory.

Anna Akhmatova

"We cannot say farewell"

We cannot say farewell,—
We just wander shoulder to shoulder.
Already it begins to darken;
You are pensive, I am still.

Into a church let's go and see
Dirges, christenings, weddings.
Not glancing at each other, let's leave . . .
Why is it just not that way with us?

Or let's sit on the flattened snow
In the graveyard, let's lightly sigh,
And with a stick you draw mansions
Where we will ever be together.

"Yes, somewhere there is a simple life and a light"

Yes, somewhere there is a simple life and a light,
Transparent, warm, and full of joy . . .
There across the fence at evening a neighbor
Talks with a girl and only the bees hear
The conversation tenderest of all.

And we live solemnly and laboriously
And honor the rites of our bitter meetings
While with a gust the foolhardy wind
Tears off a speech that has barely begun.

But for nothing would we exchange the splendid
Granite city of glory and vexation,
City of broad rivers, shining ice,
The sunless, gloomy gardens,
And the Muse's voice just faintly heard.

"How can you look at the Neva?"

How can you look at the Neva?
How can you go out on the bridge? . . .
Not for nothing do they call me sad
From the time you came in a dream.
Black angels' wings are sharp;
It will soon be the Last Judgment;
And the crimson bonfires,
Like roses, flower in the snow.

Bezhetsk

There are white churches and ringing, shining ice.
There my dear son's cornflower eyes are blooming.
Above the ancient town are diamond Russian nights
And a sickle in the sky yellower than lime-blossom honey.
There dry snowstorms fly in from fields over the river,
And people, like angels, glad at God's Holiday,
Have cleaned the light-parlor, kindled the icon lamps,
And the Blest Book lies on an oaken table.
There stern memory, so stingy now,
With a deep bow opened its tower rooms to me;
But I did not go in, I slammed shut the fearful door;
And the town was full of the joyous Christmas ringing.

Boris Pasternak

He has compared himself to a horse's eye
And looks askance, regards, sees, knows,
And lo! already with melted diamonds
Puddles are shining, ice is languishing,

In the lilac gloom backyards repose,—
Platforms, timbers, leaves, clouds.
Whistle of an engine, crunch of watermelon rind,
In fragrant kidskin a shy hand.

It rings, it thunders, it grinds, it beats with breakers,
And suddenly it goes still. It means that he
Timidly picks his way over pine needles
So as not to frighten the light sleep of space.

And it means that he is reckoning the seeds
In the blasted ears, it means that he
Has come again to the Daryal gorge,
Cursed and black, from some sort of funeral.

And there burns anew the Moscow weariness,
There ring far off the deadly sleighbells . . .
Who has got lost two steps from his house
Where snow is waist high and there's an end to all?

For having compared smoke with Laocoon,
For having sung thistles in a cemetery,
For having filled the world with a new sound
Of verses in a new space echoing,

He is rewarded with some sort of eternal childhood,
He has shone with lavishness and vigilance,
And the whole earth was his inheritance,
And he shared it out with everyone.

At Evening

The music rang in the garden
With such inexpressible grief.
They smelt fresh and sharp of the sea,
The oysters on ice in the dish.

He told me "I am a true friend!"
And gave a touch to my dress.
How little was like an embrace
In the touching of those hands!

So do they stroke a cat or a bird.
So they look at a well-built rider.
But there was laughter in his peaceful eyes
Beneath the light golden lashes.

And the voices of sorrowing violins
Sing at the smoke as it spreads:
"Give thanks indeed to the heavens:
You are the first time alone with your love."

Lot's Wife

And the just man went behind God's messenger,
Huge and shining, over the black hill.
But loudly a demand spoke to the woman.
"It is not late, you may still take a look

At the red towers of your native Sodom,
At the court where you span,
At the empty windows of the high house
Where to your dear husband you bore children!"

She glanced—and, bound by a deadly pain,
Her eyes were able to look no more;
Her body turned into transparent salt,
And her rapid feet grew into the ground.

Who will shed tears over this woman?
Does she not seem the less because of her loss?
Yet my heart never will forget
One who gave her life for a single glance.

Rachel

And Jacob served seven years for Rachel;
and they seemed unto him but a few days,
for the love he had to her.

And Jacob met Rachel in the valley;
He bowed to her like a homeless wanderer.
Flocks blew up a hot cloud of dust.
The well was blocked with an enormous stone.
He unblocked the stone with his own hand
And gave the sheep to drink of pure water.

But in his breast the heart began to mourn,
To feel pain, like an open wound,
And he agreed to serve for the girl
As a shepherd with Laban for seven years.
Rachel! For the man who was in your power,
Seven years were as seven blinding days.

But silver-loving Laban was very wise,
And pity was unknown to him.
He thinks: every deceit is forgiven
In the glory of Laban's house.
And he leads the unseeing Leah with a firm hand
To Jacob at the time for wedding.

A lofty night flows over the desert,
Chilly dews are dropping,
And the youngest daughter of Laban groans,
Rending her downy braids.
She damns her sister and reviles God,
And calls on the Angel of Death to appear.

And Jacob's dream is the hour of bliss,
The transparent spring of the valley,
The joyful look in Rachel's eyes
And her voice like a dove's:
Jacob, was it not you who kissed me
And called me with the name of your black dove?

Anna Akhmatova

"As at a meal"

As at a meal—bench, table, window
With an enormous silver moon.
We drink coffee and black wine,
We rave about music. All's the same . . .
And a branch flowers at the wall.
And in this there was a sharp sweetness,
Sweetness, if you wish, not repeatable,
Of deathless roses, dry vines.
The motherland gave us shelter.

"It lasts without end"

It lasts without end—in amber, the heavy day!
How impossible the sadness, how futile the waiting!
And once again with silver voice the deer
In the deer park speaks of the Northern Lights.
And I believed there was chilly snow,
A blue font for those who were beggars and sick,
And for a little sleigh such an unsteady run
Under the ancient ringing of the far bells.

Tashkent Is Blossoming

As though at the command of someone
At once in the city it brightened—
At every courtyard as a spectre
It entered, white and light.

And their breathing is more understood than words,
But their likeness is doomed,
Amid the sky's burning blue,
To lie in a ditch's depths.

"I will recall the roof of stars"

I will recall the roof of stars,
With the shining of eternal glories,
And the little ring-shaped rolls
Held by the dark-braided mothers
In their young hands.

"If all who for help of spirit"

If all who for help of spirit
Have begged from me in this world,
All the blest fools and mutes,
Abandoned women and cripples,
Prisoners and suicides,
Sent me a kopek apiece,—
I'd be "richer than all in Egypt"
As said Kuzmin, who rests in peace . . .
But they did not send me kopeks,
No, they shared with me their strength,
And I got stronger than all in the world.

So that *this* wearies me no more.

"There my shadow lingers and is sad"

There my shadow lingers and is sad,
Is still living in the same blue room,
Waits past midnight for a guest from town,
And kisses the small icon of enamel.
And in the house all is not wholly well:
They light a fire but still it is dark.
Isn't this why the new mistress is bored,
Isn't this why the master drinks wine
And listens how as past a thin wall
The guest, having arrived, converses with me?

Leningrad: March 1941

I awaited him in vain for many years.
That time resembled a drowsiness.
But an inextinguishable light shone forth
On Palm Sunday three years ago.
My voice broke off and went silent—
Before me with a smile stood my betrothed.

And at the window with candles the people
Went unhurriedly. O devout evening!
April's thin ice crackled gently.
And above the throng the voice of bells
Like a prophetic consolation, rang,
And a dark wind stirred up the flashes.

And white narcissi were on the table,
And a red wine in a flat goblet
I saw as though in the gloom before the dawn.
My hand, splattered upon with wax,
Trembled as it received a kiss.
And the blood sang: triumphant, blest!

"The Sundial of the House of Menshikov"

The sundial of the house of Menshikov.
Raising a wave, a steamboat passes by.
Oh, is anything on earth better known to me
Than the shine of spires, the sheen of these waters!
Like a chink the little alley stands in darkness.
The sparrows are sitting on a wire.
And of perambulations learned by heart
The salty aftertaste also gives no pain.

Secret Craftsmanship

Oh how heady is the breath of cloves,
Once on a time I had a dream of there,
There where the Eurydices are circling,
The bull carries Europa on the waves.
There where our shadows are borne along,
Upon the Neva, upon the Neva, upon the Neva;
There where the Neva plashes round the step
That is your pass to immortality.[*]

> [*]This whole poem addresses Mandelshtam. The word for "pass,"
> "propusk," echoes the same word ("I do not need a permit for the
> night") in Mandelshtam's poem, "Petersburg," printed hereafter.

Petersburg (by Osip Mandelshtam)

In Petersburg we shall unite anew
As though we had done last rites for the Sun there
And the beatific, senseless word
Had brought forth for the first time.
In the black velvet of the Soviet night,
In the velvet of the whole world's emptiness
Blest women's very own eyes are singing still.
Immortal blossoms are still blossoming.

The capital hunches, a wild cat,
Upon the bridge is standing a patrol,
Only a nasty motor tears on through the gloom
And, as a cuckoo, screeches on.
I do not need a permit for the night,
I am not frightened of the guards,
For the beatific, senseless word
I in the Soviet night shall say a prayer.

I hear the light rustle of the theatre
And the "Ah!" of maidens.
There is a huge bunch of immortal roses
That Cypris is holding in her arms.
At the bonfire we warm ourselves for boredom,
Perhaps ages will go on by.
And the very own arms of blessed women
Will gather the light ash.

Somewhere are the sweet choirs of Orpheus
And the dark pupils of their very own eyes,
And on the rows of stalls from the gallery
The playbills are falling down as doves.
So please do blow our candles out,
In the black velvet of the whole world's emptiness
Blest women's steep shoulders are singing still,
But you, you will not notice the night sun.

Anna Akhmatova

"Invisible one, double, mockingbird"

Invisible one, double, mockingbird,
Why do you hide in the black bushes,
Suddenly you start to beat your wings
Then you flit to the perished crosses.
Then you'll cry out from the Marinsky Tower:
"I returned home today,
Behold, native fields,
What has happened to me because of this.
An abyss swallowed my beloved
And my parents' home is plundered."
You and I today, Marina,
Walk through the midnight capital,
And behind us there are millions like us,
And there is no procession more wordless,
And around us funereal chimes
And Moscow's wild moans
Of a snowstorm, covering our steps.

March, 1940
(Written for Tsvetaeva)

"Oh, Muse of Weeping"
M. Tsvetaeva

... And here, I have renounced all,
Any bliss on earth,
The forest brake of branches has become
The guardian spirit of "that place."

All of us are rather guests of life.
To live is only a habit,
I hear on the air ways
The exchange of two voices.

Two? Yet still beside the eastern wall,
In the growth of a strong raspberry bush,
The dark fresh branch of the rowan—
It's a letter from Marina.

November, 1961
(at the Harbour)
(in delirium)
(from Komarovskie Sketches)

On Requiem:

Lydia Chukovskaya writes in her memoirs:

> Anna Andreevna, visiting me, would read poems from *Requiem* to me, also in a whisper, yet at her home at Fontanny Dom, she would not permit herself to do so even in a whisper; all of a sudden, in the middle of a conversation, she would fall silent and, indicating the ceiling and the walls with her gaze, would take a scrap of paper and a pencil; then, she would say something very social in a loud voice: "would you like some tea?" or "you're very suntanned," then she would write out on a scrap of paper in a rapid hand and beckon to me. I would read the poems through, and memorize them, and then return them to her in silence. "Nowadays there's such an early autumn," Anna Andreevna would say loudly and, striking a match, would burn the paper over the ashtray.
>
> This was a rite: hands, a match, an ashtray, a wonderful and sad rite.[1]

Requiem

No, not under a foreign horizon,
And not under the shelter of foreign wings,
I was then with my people,
Where, to their misfortune, my people were.

1961

In lieu of a Preface

In the terrible Yezhovschina years,[2] I spent seventeen months in prison lines in Leningrad. One time someone "recognized" me. Then a woman, with blue lips, who was standing behind me, and who of course had never heard my name, came out of the state of shock that we all felt and asked, whispering in my ear (there, everyone spoke in a whisper):

"But can you describe this?"

And I said:

"I can."

Then something resembling a smile crossed what had once been her face.

April 1, 1957
Leningrad

Dedication

Mountains bend before such grief,
The mighty river does not flow,
But bolts in prison locks are strong,
And behind them "convicts' holes"
And deadly anguish.
For someone a fresh wind is blowing,
For someone the sunset is soothing,
We don't know, we are the same everywhere,
All we hear is the hateful scrape of the keys
And the heavy steps of the soldiers.
We got up, as if for early mass,
Walked through the capital gone wild,
There we met, more lifeless than the dead,
The sun lower and the Neva mistier,
Yet hope all the while sings in the distance.
The sentence . . . And at once tears surge
Already cut off from everyone else,
As though life will be torn from the heart in pain,
As though it will be brutally thrown back,
But goes on . . . Stumbles . . . Alone . . .
Where are now the unwilling women, friends
Of my two satanic years?
What appears to them in a Siberian snowstorm,
What do they glimpse in the circle of the moon?
To them I send my greeting of farewell.

March 1940

Introduction

It was when only the dead
Smiled, glad of the peace.
And Leningrad, like an unneeded makeweight
Dangled by all of its prisons.
And when, having gone mad from torment,
The troops of those already condemned walked past,
And the train whistles were singing
A brief song of parting.
Stars of death stood above us,
And innocent Rus writhed
Under the bloodied boots
And under the tires of Black Marias.

1.

They took you away at daybreak,
I followed after you, as after your coffin,
In the dark chamber the children were crying,
The icon-case candle spilled over.
On your lips the cold of my icon,
The sweat of death on your brow . . . I will never forget!
I will, like the wives of the Streltsy,[3]
Wail by the Kremlin's towers.

1935

2.

Quietly flows the quiet Don,
A yellow moon enters the home,

Enters in a cap tossed aslant
Sees the yellow moon a shadow.

This woman is ill,
This woman's alone,

Husband in the grave, son in prison,
Pray for me.

3.

No, it's not I, it's someone else suffering.
I just could not so, and yet what has happened,
Let the black cloths cover,
And let the lamps be carried out . . .
     Night.

4.

If only I could show you, scoffer
And favorite of all my friends,
Tsarskoe Selo's cheerful sinner,
What will happen with your life—
How as the three hundredth one with a package,
You will stand by the Kresty prison,
And your burning tear
Will burn through the New Year ice.
There the prison poplar is swaying,
And no sound is heard—but there how many
Innocent lives are ending...

5.

Seventeen months have I cried out,
Calling you home.
I threw myself at the hangman's feet,
You my son and terror.
Everything has been muddled forever,
And I cannot figure out
Now, who is beast, who is human,
And how long to wait for the execution.
And only dusty flowers,
And the sound of censers, and tracks
To somewhere into nowhere.
And an enormous star
Looks directly in my eyes
And threatens with sudden destruction.

1939

6.

Lightly the weeks fly by,
What happened, I can't understand.
How the white nights looked in on you,
My son, in prison.
How they gaze once again
With a hawk's ardent eye,
Speaking about your high cross
And about death.

1939

7.
The Sentence

And the stone word fell
On my still living breast.
It's nothing, for I was ready,
I will cope with this somehow.

I have a lot to do today:
Have to finish off all trace of memory
Have to make sure that my soul's turned to stone,
Have to learn how to live again,

And yet . . . The burning rustle of summer,
Is like a holiday outside my window.
For a long time now I've had a foreboding
About this bright day and this deserted home.

Summer 1939

8.
To Death

All the same you'll come, so why not now?
I'm waiting for you—it's very hard for me.
I've put out the light, and opened up the door
For you, so simple and wondrous.
Take whatever form you like,
Tear in like a poison shell
Or sneak up with a bar-bell like a seasoned bandit,
Or poison with typhus fumes.
Or like a fairy tale, thought up by you
So familiar that everyone is sick of it,
So that I would see the blue top of a cap,
And the house manager, pale from fear.
It's all the same to me now. The Yenisei river swirls,
The North star is shining.
And a blue sparkle of beloved eyes
clouds the final terror.

August 19, 1939
Fontanny Dom

9.

Already madness with its wing
Has covered half my soul,
And gives me to drink a fiery wine
And beckons me into the dark vale.

And I understood, to it
Must I cede victory,
Listening to my own ravings
Already as if to a stranger's.

And it will not allow me
To take anything away with me
(No matter how I beg it,
No matter how I implore or plead):

Not the terrible eyes of my son—
Suffering turned to stone,
Nor the day, when the thunder came,
Nor the time of a prison visit,

Not the dear coolness of his hands,
Not the agitated shades of the lindens,
Not the remote light sound—
The words of final consolations.

May 4, 1940
Fontanny House

The Crucifixion

*"Do not weep for me, Mother,
I live in the grave."*

I

A choir of angels proclaimed the great hour,
And the heavens melted into fire.
To the Father He said:" Why hast Thou forsaken Me."
To the Mother: "Oh do not weep for Me . . . "

II

The Magdalene beat her chest and sobbed,
The Beloved disciple turned to stone,
And where the Mother stood silent,
No one even dared to glance.

1940–1943

Epilogue
I

I have come to recognize how faces age,
How out from under eyelids fear looks out,
How suffering carves cruel, cuneiform
Pages onto cheeks,
How curls of ash and ebony
Suddenly turn to silver,
A smile fades on humble lips,
And fear trembles in a faint dry snicker.
And I pray not for myself alone,
But for everyone, who stood there with me,
Both in the freezing cold, and in the July heat,
By the red blind wall.

II.

Once again the memorial hour's drawn near.
I see you, I hear you, I sense you:

And the woman, barely led up to the window,
And the one who does not trample her native earth.

And the one who shook her beautiful head,
And said: "Coming here is like coming home."

I would want to call everyone by their name,
But they've taken the list, and there's nowhere to find out.

For them have I woven a broad cloth
Out of their poor, overheard words.

I will remember them always and everywhere,
I will not forget them even in new misfortune,

And if they will close my tortured mouth,
Through which one hundred million have cried,

Let them also remember me
On the eve of my memorial day.

Yet if sometime in this country
They think of building a statue to me,

I give consent to this solemnity
But with the condition: do not build it

Near the sea, where I was born:
The last tie with the sea has long been torn,

Nor in the Tsar's garden by the cherished tree-stump,
Where an inconsolable shade is looking for me,

But here, where I 've stood for three hundred hours
And where the bolt was not drawn for me.

Since even in blessed death I'm afraid
To forget the rumbling of the Black Marias.

To forget, how the hateful door clanged
And an old woman wailed, like a wounded beast.

And let from eyelids unmoving and bronze
Melted snow stream like tears,

And let the dove in the prison coo from afar
And ships quietly sail along the Nevá.

March, 1940.

Notes

[1]Lydia Chukovskaya, *Zapiski ob Anne Akhmatovoi*, I, 10.

[2]Yezhov: known as "the bloodthirsty dwarf." Appointed People's
    Commissar for Internal Affairs in 1936, and head of the NKVD
    (National Committee of Internal Affairs); he fell from power in the
    fall of 1938, and was either imprisoned or put in an asylum and
    then executed. He also may have been charged with being a foreign
    agent. (Robert Conquest, *The Great Terror: Stalin's Purges of the
    Thirties*. New York: Macmillan, 1968).

[3]Streltsy: The Palace Guards Regiment who supported Empress Sophia
    and were executed at the Kremlin walls by Peter the Great.

Bibliography

Introduction

Bannikov, Nikolai, ed. *Russkie poetessy XIX Veka*. Moscow: Sovetskaya Rossiia. 1979.

Bukhshtab, V. Ya. ed. *Poety 1840-1850kh godov*. Moscow, Leningrad: Biblioteka Poeta; Sovetskii Pisatel'. 1962.

Conquest, Robert. *The Great Terror: Stalin's Purge of the Thirties*. New York: Macmillan, 1968.

Gray, Francine du Plessis. *Soviet Women: Walking the Tightrope*. New York: Doubleday, 1990.

Uchenova, V.V. "Zabveniu vopreki: Tvorchestvo russkikh isatel'nits pervoi poloviny XIX veka," introd. *Dacha na Petergofskoi doroge: Proza russkikh pisatel'nits pervoi polovinoi XIX veka* Moscow: Sovremennik, 1986.

Akhmatova

Akhmatova, Anna. *Sochineniia*. G. P. Struve and B. A. Filippov, eds. Munich: Inter-Language Literary Associates, 1967. 2 vols.

Akhmatova, Anna. *Sochineniia v dvukh tomakh*. Introd. M. Dudin, ed. V. A. Cherny. Moscow: Khudozhestvennaya Literatura, 1986.

Akhmatova, Anna. *Rekviem: 1935-1940*. G. Struve, ed. New York: Tovarischestvo Zarubezhnykh Pisatelei, 1969.

Chukovskaya, Lydia. *Zapiski ob Anne Akhmatovoi, Vol. 1. 1938-1941*. Paris: YMCA Press, 1976.

Driver, Sam. *Anna Akhmatova*. New York: Twayne's World Authors Series, 198. 1972.

Driver, Sam. "Anna Akhmatova: Theory and Practice." Canadian-American Slavic Studies, 22, Nos. 1-4. 1988. 343-351.

Khrenkov, Dmitri. *Anna Akhmatova: v Peterburge —Petrograde — Leningrade*. Leningrad: Lenizdat, 1989.

Bunin

Bannikov, Nikolai, ed. *Russkie poetessy XIX Veka*. Moscow: Sovetskaya Rossiia. 1979.

Gippius

Gippius, Zinaidea. *Stikhotvorenii i Poemy*. Tamira Pachmuss, ed. Munich: Fink, 1972.

Lokhvitskaya

Lokhvitskaya, M. A. *Stikhotvoreniia*. Moscow, 1896.
Stikhotvoreniia:: 1896-1898. vol. 2., Moscow, 1898.
Stikhotvoreniia: 1898-1900. vol. 3. St. Petersburg, 1900.
Stikhotvoreniia: 1900-1902: vol. 4., St. Petersburg, 1902.
Stikhotvoreniia: 1902-1904. St. Petersburg, 1904.
Iz russkoi Lirikoi, No. 17. Berlin: Mysl'. 1921.
Pachmuss, Temira A. "Lokhvitskaya," *A Handbook of Russian Literature*, ed. Victor Terras. Yale UP. 263-4.
Terras, Victor. *A History of Russian Literature*. London and New Haven: Yale UP, 1991.

Parnok

Parnok. Sophia. *Sobranie Stikhotvorenii.* , ed. and introd. by Sophia Poliakova. Ann Arbor: Ardis, 1979.
Lang, Anna. "Parnok," *A Handbook of Russian Literature*, ed. Victor Terras, 330.
Poliakova, Sophia. *Zakatnye ony dni: Tsvetaeva i Parnok*. Ann Arbor: Ardis, 1983.

Pavlova

Bukhshtab, V. Ya. *Poety 1840-1850kh godov*. Moscow, Leningrad: Biblioteka Poeta; Sovetskii Pisatel'. 1962.
Heldt, Barbara. "Karolina Pavlova: "The Woman and the Double Life."introd. *A Double Life*. Oakland. Barbary Coast Books. 1986.
Pavlova, Karolina. *Polnoe Sobranie Stikhotvoreniia*, introd., P. P. Gromov, ed. M. Gaidankov Moscow, Leningrad: Sovetskii Pisatel'. 1964.

Rostopchina

Rostopchina, Evdokia P. *Sochineniia grafini E. P. Rostopchinoi s eia portretom*. St. Petersburg: Tipografia I. N. Skorokhodova. 1890. Biographical Sketch by Sergei Sushkov. I. Stikhi. II. Proza.
Ernst, S. "Karolina Pavlova i gr. Evodkia Rostopchina." *Russkii Bibliofil'* No. 6. Petrograd: 1916. 5-35.
Terras, Victor."Rostopchiná." *Handbook of Russian Literature*, ed. Victor Terras. New Haven and London: Yale UP, 1985.
Bannikov, Nikolai, ed. *Russkie poetessy XIX Veka*. Moscow: Sovetskaya Rossiia. 1979.

Shkapskaya

Shkapskaya, Maria M. *Stikhi*. Introd. essays by B. Filippov and E. Zhiglevich. London: 1979.

Filippov, Boris. "Shkápskaya." *Handbook of Russian Literature*, ed. Victor Terras. New Haven and London: Yale U P, 1985. 406-407.

Solovieva

Bannikov, Nikolai, ed. *Russkie poetessy XIX Veka*. Moscow: Sovetskaya Rossiia. 1979.

Teplova

Bannikov, Nikolai, ed. *Russkie poetessy XIX Veka*. Moscow: Sovetskaya Rossiia. 1979.

Tsvetaeva

Tsvetaeva, Marina. *Izbrannaia Proza v dvukh tomakh: 1917-1937*. Alexander Sumerkin, Ed. New York: Russica, Inc, 1979.

Tsvetaeva, Marina. *Stikhotvoreniia i poemy v pyati tomakh*. Ed. Alexander Sumarkin. NY: Russica, 1980.

Tsvetaeva, Marina. *Sochineniia v dvukh tomakh*. Ed. Anna A. Saakiants, Moscow: Khudozhestvennaya Literatura. 1988.

Tsvetaeva, Marina. *Pisma k Anne Teskovoi*, Ed. Vadim Markovin, Prague, Jerusalem: Versty, 1982.

Tsvetaeva, Marina. "Popytka Komnaty." *Volia Rossii*, 1928.

Tsvetaeva, Marina. *A Captive Spirit: Selected Prose*, Ed. and trans. J. Marin King. Ann Arbor: Ardis, 1980.

Zvétaieva, Marina. *Mon frére féminin : lettre à l'Amazone*. Paris: Mercure de France, 1979.

Izvolskaya, Elena. "Ten na stenakh." *Opyty*, III.

Karlinsky Marina Tsvetaeva: *The Woman, her World and her Poetry*. Cambridge: Cambridge University Press, 1985.

Karlinsky, Simon. *Marina Cvetaeva: Her Life and Art* Berkeley: U of California Press, 1966.

Losskaya, Veronika. *Marina Tsvetaeva v zhizni: Neizdannye vospominanija sovremennikov* Hermitazh:, 1989.

Saakiants, Anna A. *Marina Tsvetaeva: Strrannitsy zhizni i tvorchestva (1910-1922)*, Moscow: Sovetskii Pisatel', 1986.

Schweitzer, Victoria. *Byt' i Bytie Mariny Tsvetaevoii*. Paris: Sintaksis, 1988.

Taubman, Jane. *A Life Through Poetry: Marina Tsvetaeva's Lyric Diary*. Columbus: Slavica Publishers, 1989.

Pasternak, Boris. Tsvetaeva, Marina. Rilke, Rainer Maria. *Letters: Summer 1926*, trans. Walter Arndt, Margaret Wettlin, eds. Yevgeni Pasternak, Yelena Pasternak, Konstantin M. Azadovsky. New York: Harcourt Brace Johanovich, 1985.

Pasternak, Boris. Tsvetaeva, Marina. Rilke, Rainer Maria. *Pis'ma 1926 goda* Eds. K. M. Azadovsky, E. B. Pasternak, E. V. Pasternak. Moscow: Kniga, 1990.

Zubova, L. V. *Poezia Mariny Tsvetaevoi: Lingvisticheskii aspekt.* Leningrad: Leningrad UP, 1989.

Zhadovskaya

Bannikov, Nikolai, ed. *Russkie poetessy XIX Veka.* Moscow: Sovetskaya Rossiia. 1979.

Bukhshtab, V. Ya. *Poety 1840-1850kh godov.* Moscow, Leningrad: Biblioteka Poeta; Sovetskii Pisatel'. 1962.

DATE DUE

GAYLORD   PRINTED IN U.S.A.